WHAT DOES IT MEAN TO BE
BORN AGAIN

WHAT DOES IT MEAN TO BE

BORN AGAIN

John Wesley White
Foreword by Billy Graham

Bethany Fellowship INC.
MINNEAPOLIS, MINNESOTA 55438

What Does It Mean To Be Born Again?
by John Wesley White

Library of Congress Catalog Card Number

ISBN 0-87123-641-9

Copyright © 1977
Bethany Fellowship, Inc.
All Rights Reserved

DIMENSION BOOKS
Published by Bethany Fellowship, Inc.
6820 Auto Club Road, Minneapolis, Minnesota 55438

Printed in the United States of America

DR. JOHN WESLEY WHITE is an evangelist in the Billy Graham organization. He is also Chancellor of Richmond College, Toronto, Ontario, Canada, and the host and speaker for "Agape," a half-hour weekly television program broadcast across North America.

He makes his home, with his wife and family, in Willowdale, Ontario.

He was educated at Moody Bible Institute, received his B.A. from Wheaton College, and continued his education at Queens, Trinity, and Oxford, England. He took his D.Phil. from Oxford.

His evangelistic efforts have taken him to 100 nations of the world, and he has addressed an aggregate of two and one-half million people concerning the Gospel, and has seen some one hundred thousand of them indicate commitments to Christ.

He has written eight other books prior to this one.

Foreword

The author of this book is John Wesley White, who has served as one of my Associate Evangelists for 14 years. Born in Saskatchewan, Canada, and now residing in Toronto, he was educated in five countries, culminating the earning of a doctor of philosophy degree from Oxford University in England. Since coming with me, he has been to a hundred countries in every part of the world. He has preached to crowds as large as thirty-five thousand and praises the Lord for having seen some one hundred thousand come forward to make decisions for Christ. Chancellor of Richmond College, he has also served as its hockey coach, where his four sons have been enrolled. His wife, Kathleen, is Irish. For three years he has been the speaker on our weekly TV program, "Agape," a ministry of the Billy Graham Evangelistic Association.

To those of you who are Christians, I hope that the reading of this book will arouse you to a new zeal in evangelism. To those of you who are not, I trust you will respond to God's promise: "Whosoever shall call upon the name of the Lord shall be saved."

Billy Graham
Montreat, NC
June, 1977

Preface

In "Jesus of Nazareth," the most promoted and viewed religious film ever presented on television, captivating an audience of 43 million North Americans, more was made of Jesus' encounter with Nicodemus than of any other single event except for the crucifixion. The "born again" encounter of John 3 and the stand which Nicodemus took in chapter 7 before the Jewish hierarchy were both highlighted. And when Jesus was on His cross, Nicodemus stood at the base, looking up and exclaiming with tremendous emotion and meaning, "Born again! Born again!"

On the leading Canadian Broadcasting Company radio show "As It Happened," Barbara Frum was interviewing Washington Post Correspondent Nicholas Von Hoffman in March, 1977. She asked him about the new book on Gerald Ford's life. "It'll bomb," he predicted, just as those on Nixon, Johnson and every other professional politician since John Kennedy have bombed. There was one exception—Chuck Colson's *Born Again*. Von Hoffman said he didn't "buy" its message, but for some peculiar reason, it's rolled over this continent like a prairie fire.

Though nearly 2,000 years old, the phrase "born again," either suspect or strangely irrelevant prior to these late 1970's, has appeared in the table talk of North Americans. You hear it on "The Morning Show," "The Today Show," "The Tonight Show" and "The Tomorrow Show." It's a cover-story grabber for *Time, Newsweek, People* and *U.S. News and World Report.* It's the theme of pollsters, politicians and pundits. "Dear Abby" gets a letter from "Born Again." And her sister Ann Landers' "writer in" has decided to go back to the mother of his illegitimate baby and marry her, because being born again has given him new love as well as a new sense of responsibility. A tragic suicide by a Hollywood actress was allegedly preceded by "I only wish I could be born again!" A Canadian celebrity takes LSD and exclaims in retrospect: "I felt like I was born again, only the next morning I felt like hell."

Nor is the "born again" happening confined to Protestants. Archbishop Fulton Sheen says candidly that there simply is no doubt about it: the foremost current need of Americans is to re-read and act responsively on the command of Jesus of Nazareth: "You must be born again."

So, what does it mean to be *born again*?

Table of Contents

Chapter 1

Why All the Attention To Being Born Again?

Why all the sudden attention to people wanting to be born again?

To begin with, universal man is acutely aware that he's into the birthpangs of a life-and-death struggle to be born. Harold I. Ickes has put it: "The travail of the world is on." Man is at the stage of an unemerged baby bird, pecking desperately on the inside of his shell, instinctively resolved to break out into that world of sunshine, fresh air, food, freedom and fulfillment. He feels enclosed in a cocoon. The time for his butterflying forth has to be now.

Man is trying desperately to simulate life, when in fact he feels himself being overtaken on his blindside by death. He finds himself trapped—like trying to pick up ashes with a table fork in a windy Sahara when he's actually craving to be picking up oranges in Orlando. Instead he feels swindled and ripped off, exiled to some psychological Siberian salt mine.

As Mr. Nixon said in his last interview with David Frost, the deadest, most lonely and bored people on earth are the affluent pleasure seekers, lolling endlessly in the glamorous watering places of the south coast of France or the east coast of Florida, going from golf course to cocktail lounge to bridge party, but never having found any vital purpose for living. Joan Kennedy wept for a whole world of wealth and fame when she allegedly blurted out: "Dear God, where has all the happiness gone?" She was soon to be joined by Princess Margaret of Britain and Margaret Trudeau of Canada.

One of Canada's most visible and revered intellectuals is McGill Professor and broadcaster Laurier Lapierre. He discloses his personal despair, as quoted in a national magazine: "There are so many nights when I go to bed and I really think it would be so much better if I didn't wake up the next morning. The first thing I say to myself in the morning is 'why?' I get into my car and say it would be nice if someone were to run into me and I went through the windshield." From the professor in his ivory tower to the student world, the mood is not different. In a recent poll, 78% of American university students "felt their lives were meaningless." Nor is it different in the world of contrived laughter. Perhaps the world's best known female commedian cries: "I want to quit, even to kill myself." Superstar Jennifer O'Neill laments: "Being beautiful is a curse." Ringo Starr, the Beatle, is singing: "Oh no, no, no I can't take it no more!" A CBC celebrity says on a network show: "I think it's a battle just to stay alive!" An American, like so many in her profession, who is going regularly to a psychiatrist, is Joanne Woodward, the beautiful actress wife of Paul Newman. She laments: "A lot of mornings I can hardly make myself get out from under the covers and try to be me. I've had times when I figured the best thing Paul could do with me is to take me out the back and shoot me like a crippled horse. That's how fulfilled and complete I am."

It sometimes seems that the who's who in today's world are about as alive as the figures in Madame Tussaud's wax museum in London. A book on Janis Joplin has been published entitled *Buried Alive.* Actually her real problem was that she was "dead in trespasses and sins" (Eph. 2:1). The Bible also puts it: "She that liveth in pleasure is dead while she liveth" (1 Tim. 5:6). The ancient king Solomon sought fulfillment in mirth, money and mindism. One of the wealthiest, wisest and most swinging personalities of that half of history known as B.C., he ended up writing a letter to his sons, in which he regretted: "Therefore I hated life" (Eccles. 2:17). This was in spite of his 700 wives, 300 concubines—and all the saddle horses and chariot drags of ancient history's gloriana kicks. But there was the kickback! Like millions of moderns, Solomon was all vogue on the outside, but all vague on the inside: or as Richard Chamberlain the actor laments: "I'm laughing on the outside but crying on the inside."

Someone else who was laughing on the outside but crying on the inside, obviously, was Freddie Prinz who drove that killer bullet through his head. Watched by 1 in 7 North Americans that week on "Chico and the Man," the 22-year-old youth god had just gotten off the telephone with his mother—and his wife. It was 4 a.m.! At one side was his manager, and at the other his psychiatrist. Freddie shocked his following with a shot that was heard in screaming headlines around the world. The life of the party, he was dead inside.

Nor are these just isolated instances. Suicide on this Continent among under 19-year-olds, according to Catholic Archbishop Fulton Sheen, doubled in two years. Ann Landers has the impression from her 80 million readers that among all North Americans, if all the facts were in, only heart failure, cancer, and alcohol-related deaths would be ahead of suicide as a killer. My wife, Kathleen, brought me the newspaper the other day with the remark: "Another suicide!" It was a front pager. On page 3 there was another gory story of yet another poor soul taking his own life. *Homemakers* magazine opens a feature article with the agonizing fact: "In the past two years, the number of suicides among teenagers has tripled. "Why?" demands Brenda Rabkin, "are so many of our young people turning to death as the only way out?" Dr. H. B. Cotnam, Ontario's supervising coroner, announces: "Teenage suicides, some involving 14-year-olds, tripled in Metro Toronto last year." Throughout North American society, suicide has leapt into second place as a killer of 14- to 30-year-olds. And, it is an even higher per capita killer of men over 65 years of age. One day it seems to be an Eastern king, taking an overdose; the next, a teenage idol: Gram Parsons; or it may be TV's former "Family Affair" starlette Mary Anissa Jones, who played Buffy; or it may be another Jim Croce, or a Jimi Hendrix. It's become a theatre theme, with titles like: "Death Wish," "Death Sentence," and "The Suicide."

University of Massachusetts psychology professor Brian Mishara reckons that two out of three of our young today get so low on downers, at one time or another, that they think of ending their lives by their own hand. He says that many car crash fatalities are not accidents at all, but suicides, a fact that was demonstrated here in Southwestern Ontario recently when a teenager, whose girlfriend jilted him, floor-boarded his car and at a hundred miles an hour killed six other young people with him. Heart specialist and lecturer, Dr. Henry Blackburn, reckons that masses of people today find life so intolerable that they deliberately smoke, drink, overeat, and sexualize promiscuously as if they want to get the whole swindle of human existence over and done with. He insists that the total swinger scene today is a reflection of the current revolt against life syndrome. Syndicated columnist Sydney Harris makes it clear that the statistics are conclusive. More whites than blacks per capita; more rich than poor; more swingers than squares; more foot loose and fancy singles than fettered marrieds; more educated than illiterates; more in sunshine and springtime than in the shadows or the snows; more in times of prosperity than in depression—commit suicide. So the whole crazy pattern reads, in the words of a *Toronto Star* editorial: "For the past five years the suicide rate in Metro has been rising steadily and no one knows why."

Some things we do know. It is not the poor, the illiterate or the socially oppressed who lead in the suicide spiral upwards. According to the House of Lords in England, which carried out a Royal Commission on the sharp rise of suicide in Britain, 8 times as many rich as poor; 8 times as many swingers as squares, and 8 times as many intellectuals per capita, as modestly educated, take their own lives. In fact, when I was at Oxford 15 years ago, that university had the highest suicide rate of any community in England. Reduced to a theorem, these facts read something like this: the more you earn, and the more you learn, and the more you burn, the more you yearn for life. Or in today's secular society, the more you do, the more you have and the more you know, the less fulfilled you seem to be.

Psychiatrist Dr. Jack Leedy says that everywhere today "people are disillusioned with life. They are bored with politics, bored with permissiveness, bored with violence on TV. And that's very dangerous—because it is a well-known fact in psychiatric circles that boredom can kill." It might be better stated that boredom is not so much a killer as it is evidence of people longing to come alive—to be born again. The world renowned British scientist and author, C. P. Snow, states: "People need a purpose, and purpose is one thing an affluent society hasn't been able to provide. Religion gives purpose, but in a secular age that is gone. Men and women are desperately trying to find a purpose for themselves. Without it, life is peculiarly empty."

Right here is one of the reasons why suddenly there has been an upsurge in the numbers of people worldwide who are being born again. Aimless, purposeless, unfulfilled they are turning to Christ. A most meaningful letter to come to our Agape Office in Winnipeg was this one which *Decision* magazine published verbatim. It was from a man on the West Coast who wrote: "Last May 23 on a Sunday, while I was alone in my apartment, depressed, hung over from the previous night's activities, fed up with life, trying to find a way out of it, I turned on the television set for want of something better to do. John Wesley White was just beginning the message about the vast emptiness that exists in the lives of those persons without God. This was my problem, so I began to listen. When the invitation was given to me to pray, I did—and praise the Lord, He saved me instantly. He made a new person out of me. I have been so happy that I cannot contain myself.

"I am an airline captain and I have told most of the people I work with about my experience with God. I am praying that I may be able to lead many of them to Christ. In all the years I have been flying, I can truly say that I have never been any higher than I am now with Jesus in my heart. The program 'Agape' was the vehicle God used to bring me to Him."

Another reason for the resurgence in new births is the fear that people have, worldwide, of nuclear war. St. Peter prophesied that "the day of the Lord will come as a thief in the night; in the which the heavens shall pass away with a great noise, and the elements shall melt with fervent heat, the earth also and the works that are therein shall be burned up. Seeing then that all these things shall be dissolved, what manner of persons ought ye to be?" (2 Pet. 3:10, 11).

"Fear is in the saddle, riding us all to distraction," notes a world leader. The father of the Russian hydrogen bomb, Andrei Sakharov, laments, "The unchecked growth of thermo nuclear arsenals and the build-up toward confrontation threaten mankind with the death of civilization and physical annihilation." The U.S. has 30,000 hydrogen bombs, comparable to the Russians' stockpile, we're told, and they together could exterminate man thousands of times over. The U.S. President tells Congress that by 1985 forty countries will have their own nuclear stockpiles. And guerrilla groups! Carlos, the Venezuelan terrorist, master mind of a whole chain of high-jackings (including the 100-hostage one to Uganda), is reportedly on the loose, with his own private A-bomb. The thought of such high-jackings and nuclear blackmailing is simply too terrible to anticipate.

Canada's best-known intellectual, Professor Marshall McLuhan, recently was quoted around the world as saying that nearly every other human problem is irrelevant until we've solved this matter of stopping World War III: "The Apocalypse is at hand . . . we're on the verge—on the very verge of another human slaughter." The late Albert Schweitzer reckoned: "Man has lost the capacity to foresee and to forestall. He will end by destroying the earth." Columnist Robert Fulford syndicates his opinion that: "We are all of us dedicated, in one way and another, to keeping the truth about the world at a distance," because the news of the world today is holocaust, disaster and doom.

When Barbara Walters, "the million dollar woman," was about to join Harry Reasoner on ABC's Evening News, the network promoted in advance: "The news the world has been waiting for." But alas, when they got teamed up, most of the news was bad news. Loyd Robertson, perhaps Canada's best-known newsman, was asked at the beginning of the year what his new year's resolution was. His reply: "I want to bring some good news to the people this year. Last year seemed flooded with such rotten news." A sportswriter lamented the other day: "Sportswriters are just like other people in that they don't like to listen to 'bad news.' " But good news from today's world seems on the wane. News roundups inevitably, are more and more focusing on wars and rumors of wars. A Carolina newscaster said to Leighton Ford that after most of his evening newscasts he feels so down that he wants to say: "Shall we pray!"

Consequently, since this world is passing, people are looking for the life that lasts. If "once born" means being born to die, and "twice born" means to live here and hereafter, many are saying, "Let's be born again. Let's get right with God." Billy Graham tells us that after World War II, 35% of the American scientists believed in a personal God: today it's 60%. This is largely because they know that only God can solve the dilemmas facing man today, many of which they themselves have created.

I remember when Barry McGuire sang "Eve of Destruction" to the top of the pop charts throughout the free world. It was one of those "man is doomed" songs. Then Barry had an experience of Christ and was born again. Today he is singing of how Jesus is the only way to cope with living on a planet in eclipse.

In the late sixties I held a crusade in the San Francisco Bay area, when hippiedom was emerging. A Presbyterian clergyman's son, Abner Cook, was into the subculture. But he found it to be a nowhere trip. One Wednesday night I was preaching on the Second Coming of Christ and the end of the age. Here was help and hope in a despairing and disintegrating world where man, any day, might press the self-destruct button. So Abner came forward that night and surrendered his life to Christ. I was back crusading in the Bay area again recently, and Abner came up to tell me that since that night he's been a new person. He had been born again.

Recently I was preaching to one of Florida's largest church congregations on a Sunday morning on this theme of war and the Second Coming of Christ. It was carried on television. Charles Toombs, 90 years old, and Mrs. Toombs sat at home and listened. That day they gave themselves to Christ, and in the evening came to the crusade meeting to come forward and confess Jesus Christ as Lord. Now they were ready for either Christ's coming again or His home call to them through death.

St. Peter gave us that terrible prediction of holocaust and apocalypse. But he also prophesied: "And it shall come to pass in the last days, saith God, I will pour out my Spirit upon all flesh. . . . And it shall come to pass, that whosoever shall call on the name of the Lord shall be saved" (Acts 2:17, 21). So, while masses of people are being driven toward spiritual rebirth by fear—even terror—they are also being pulled by the current outpouring of the Holy Spirit. George Gallup, Jr., the pollster, states that in the late seventies, 34% of the American people profess to have had a born-again experience, whereas a dozen years ago, it was 23%. That means an additional 30 million Americans today are saying they are born-again Christians, as compared to ten years ago.

In March, 1977, Billy Graham reckoned that Americans currently are seeing the most meaningful evangelical revival in 120 years. Certainly *Redbook* indicates that view, from its polling of 65,000 American women. An astonishing 96% believe in God, 95% believe the Bible is inspired, 91% believe God hears our prayers, 87% believe in miracles, 84% believe in life after death, 82% believe in angels, 78% believe in an actual devil, and 77% believe they've had a religious experience which is determinative in their lives. The *Redbook* pollsters confessed that they were frankly amazed at the results.

Nor is this spiritual awakening confined to North America. Leighton Ford, who as Chairman of the Lausanne Continuation Committee is constantly in touch with spiritual renewal throughout the world, states that in 1977 there are 55,000 people professing to be born again, every day, the largest response in the history of Christendon, and that 1400 new churches are being formed every week. What often doesn't come through in the secular media news is that in countries like Uganda, while Idi Amin has slaughtered a third of a million, there are more conversions taking place than ever. Churches and open-air meetings are packed. Over half of the country's population currently reckon themselves to be Christians.

We in Canada fear greatly the disintegration of our country because of what has been happening in Quebec. Yet there are some signs of hope. The correspondents Tom Harper and Les Tarr have been writing extensively about the Catholic Charismatic movement which has been penetrating French Canada. It is a most unusual movement of the Holy Spirit. There are 45,000 people meeting in 1,100 prayer groups, with as many as 20,000 having been gathered together at one time in Quebec City. Father Jean-Paul Regimbal leads 10,000 of these—and among his most enthusiastic adherents is the brilliant Jerome Choquette, former Minister of Justice—for the province of Quebec.

There is no doubt that two men are largely responsible for the emergence of the phrase "born again" among the masses. First to trumpet this phrase in the media was Charles Colson. Colson's best seller *Born Again* has on its cover two profiles of this former White House hatchet man: the one in the background is dark, grim and gloomy—like the shadows in which Colson had lived. The same face is in the foreground, only this time Colson is gleaming in living color. The message which beams out is unmistakable: Charles Colson has been "born again." Across the U.S. and Canada, the U.K. and Scandinavia especially, Colson's turning to Christ has been featured on radio and television and in the newspapers and magazines. Here was, as *Time* put it, the once "tough, wily, nasty and (so) tenaciously loyal to Richard Nixon" White House hatchet man: the one who said that he'd run over his own grandmother to get Mr. Nixon re-elected. Now he had been "born again." However did it happen? Well, he had moved out of Washington and into a wilderness world of wealth in New York City, making an enormous amount of money as head of an attorney firm. But he was bored and burdened with guilt. So he drove up to his native Boston to see his old friend Tom Phillips. I was with Billy Graham in Madison Square Gardens, New York, when New England's most successful businessman, Tom Phillips, came forward to be born again. Now it was six years later. And by night (the time Nicodemus came to Jesus) Chuck Colson went to see Tom Phillips! That evening he opened his heart to Christ. He was born again! Not merely inspired by getting a handle on a new philosophy, Colson had well and truly enthroned Jesus Christ as his Lord. He unmistakably had undergone a total transformation. It meant telling the truth about his role in Watergate to the judge, and consequently, a term in jail. But Colson was highly credible. Most people believed his story. And through his testimony thousands were led into being born again, while millions sat up and took notice.

The other man responsible for the emergence of the phrase "born again" is President Jimmy Carter, currently the most powerful man on earth. When he was elected, newspapers throughout the world featured the most conspicuous thing about him—that he was, in his own words, "born again in Christ." Oh, he had been a church member for a third of a century. But he was not yet born again. Church membership for President Carter had been a tradition, not a transformation; a dutiful religion, not a personal reality; an endurance, not an enjoyment. He was externally conformed, not internally transformed. The Bible says: "Be not conformed to this world: but be ye transformed by the renewing of your mind" (Rom. 12:2). Ten years ago, Jimmy Carter of Plains, Georgia—by his own testimony— was a disgruntled, guilty, empty, confused, lost soul who had just failed in an attempt to become Governor of his state. I happened to be there at the time of that gubernatorial race and I remember it well.

Then came that momentous Sunday afternoon in October 1967. The future U.S. President's sister Ruth, an evangelist, and Jimmy Carter, peanut farmer, went for a walk into the woods. She told him that what he needed was to surrender his life to Christ. Kneeling down together in the falling leaves and pine needles, there were tears falling from their faces. James Earle Carter asked Jesus Christ to become his personal Saviour and Lord. When he stood up again, as he has so often said since, he was truly "born again in Christ." That didn't end his problems or temptations. But it assured him a Saviour who had promised never to leave him nor forsake him. Jesus Christ would be with him always—to the White House and to the end of the world.

Chapter 2

Why Be Born Again?

When Nicodemus came to Jesus by night and asked Him who He was and what He was doing in this world, Jesus had one thing to say to him: "Ye must be born again" (John 3:7). Jesus did not say: "I venture to suggest that under certain extenuating circumstances it could be quite a good idea, Nicodemus, if you were to consider, as one of the options for your spiritual therapy, that you might conceivably contemplate the possibility of going as far as being born again." That was not what Jesus said. Instead, He commanded with all the authority and compassion of Deity: "Ye *must* be born again." *Indeed, unless you are born again, you simply "cannot enter into the kingdom of God"* (v. 5). Nicodemus must have beeen blinking! He just couldn't see it. Many a modern says: "I just can't see it." Jesus said: "Except a man be born again, he cannot see the kingdom of God" (v. 3). Nicodemus was a straight-laced blueblood, a real culture vulture from the hoi poloi of society. He was morally as clean as a hound's tooth and ecclesiastically just as sharp. His name meant "superior man." He could look down his nose at the masses.

Yet when he came to Jesus by night, craving to know the route into the Kingdom of God, Jesus said, obviously to his amazement, "Marvel not that I said unto thee, Ye *must* be born again" (v. 7).

Nicodemus was Jewish. Would a Jew need to be born again? He was a Pharisee. If he were a Saducee, the born-again bit might have made sense. Saducees believed neither in a resurrection nor the coming of the Messiah. But the Pharisees believed in both. They were orthodox. They were "fundamentalists." Nicodemus was a devout Pharisee. Despite this, Jesus said: "Ye must be born again." And he was a "ruler," one of the Sanhedrin of 71. Surely this would exempt him. But no way! There was no getting around it. There were no loopholes. There was no escape. Three times Jesus said to Nicodemus that he simply had to be born again.

Nicodemus did not act impulsively. He liked to think about something before getting his act together. But he took Jesus at His word and he was born again. This we discover in John 7:50 where we read that he took his stand for Christ. Yes, he was a believer in Jesus. And before his fellow rulers, he declared himself.

As North Americans take up this phrase "born again," it is imperative that it not become a passing fad, the latest edition of doing your own thing—like, say, TM, ESP, EST, HPM or an eccentric pursuit of UFO's, none of which involve personal repentance from sin and resignation to the holiness of God. You see, God's holiness demands that we be born again. Without "holiness," states Hebrews 12:14, "no man shall see the Lord." We are born again "that we might be partakers of his holiness" (v. 10).

The comedian Patrick Henry was appearing on Johnny Carson's "Tonight Show," when he asked a very relevant question: "How is it that everyone wants to go to heaven, yet everyone wants booze, sex, and gambling?" The Word of God clearly teaches that you can't impenitently practice these sins and go to heaven.

In a Crusade which it was my privilege to conduct in Notre Dame's ACC stadium in 1975, a beautiful Jewess gave her life to Christ. She had been born in Czechoslovakia in the 1930's. During World War II she was seized by Hitler and sent to a concentration camp in Poland. She narrowly escaped the gas chamber and after World War II, suffered untold cruelty in Russia and East Germany. In the fifties she dramatically escaped through the Iron Curtain to Holland, where she married an American army officer. By 1975, though she was financially well off, she was completely unfulfilled. I spoke on "For to me to live is Christ" and she responded to the invitation to be born again.

But as I learned later she had had, in addition to her husband, a wealthy "lover" in Florida, who would send her return airfare tickets to come and be with him. After her professing to be born again, she took her ticket and went out to the airport. She got in line. Suddenly it struck her: "What am I doing in this line? I've been born again. Christ is my Lover! I'm His!" And she returned the ticket to its purchaser in Florida. You see, as Jesus said to the ancient Jew, Nicodemus, "that which is born of the flesh is flesh; and that which is born of the Spirit is spirit" (John 3:6), so He re-affirmed to this modern Jewess.

Two years after being born again, she attended Billy Graham's great crusade in Notre Dame. With her were her two teen-aged sons. Both went forward to be born again. And her husband, Jack, in a Sunday morning service made his decision for Christ.

Why be born again? Because man's depravity demands it! I was driving along Bayview Avenue in Toronto recently and came up behind a white van, which was really filthy. A wag had finger written in the dirt: "Wash me!" The Bible teaches that man needs washing, for his nature is sinful. Men, wrote the Psalmist (14:3), "are all gone aside, they are all together become filthy: there is none that doeth good, no, not one."

You can drive up the main street of nearly any city in the Western world and only the wording in the advertisements changes from year to year, except that they keep getting more daring. The gaudiest lights advertise the most godless garbage: "Dirty Mary," "Dirty Harry," "The Dirty Dolls," "The Pig Keeper's Daughter," "The Bed Bunnies," "Carnal Knowledge," "Carnal Madness," "The Joys of Jezebel," "Frustrated Wives." "They live for love, they play for pleasure, they party for pure passion." What these wholesalers of moral trash fail to publicize is that they mean "impure" for "pure," and that they should be spelling love—L-U-S-T!

The movie "Drum" packs them in by advertising: "It lusts. It scalds. It shocks. It whips. It bleeds. It out-Mandingos Mandingo!" Many people are not aware that in both Canada and the U.S. today, both in theaters and on late night movies, masses —especially the young—are watching actual scenes of visible fornication, adultery, incest, sodomy, rape, masturbation, group sex orgies, homosexual and lesbian acts, bestiality, fellatio, connilingus, sadomasochism, people defecating, urinating, and vomiting on each other plus verbal obscenities and profanities such as would have shocked a meeting of the Mafia a decade ago. I wish that with their glamorous use of words like zany and kinky, the movie moguls would use ones like miserable, guilty, empty and regret. It's claimed that 31% of the students of a prominent university are living together outside wedlock, most with no intention of being married. We're told that only 25% of today's students think homosexuality is morally wrong, and that the percentage of those who think that premarital sex is wrong has dropped since 1969 from 57% to 34%.

Pope Paul says that we live in a time of unbridled exaltation of sex. Top pop songs of the late seventies, according to *Time*, include taunting teasers like: "You Sexy Thing," "Evil Woman," "Do It Any Way You Wanna," "Let's Do It Again," and "I Want'a Do Something Freaky to You." We're told there are now more Massage Parlors and Body Shops in our cities than McDonald's Hamburger outlets—with common names like: "Ecstasy Unlimited," "The Velvet Touch," and "This Is Heaven." Book titles entice the public: "The Joy of Sex," "Sex: The Most Fun You Can Have Without Laughing," and "All You Wanted To Know About Sex but Were Afraid To Ask." Blue movies are at the twist of the television dial, while you can go down to the cinema or the outdoor theater and see: "Sexual Fantasies," "Sex Shuffle," "Girls Who Always Say Yes," "Erotic Dreams," "Girls of Erotica," and "Let's Do It Again." It's really no wonder that a John Hopkins University study of American teenage sex mores reveals in April 1977 that 30% more American teenage girls are engaging in premarital sex activity than five years ago. Nor is it surprising that the *New York Times* reckons from a poll of 100,000 North American women that in this final quarter of the 20th century, 80% of females engage in premarital sex—90% of those under 25 years of age. More than a third of these say they have had sex with 2 to 5 men. The Kinsey Report in 1953 found that only 33% of women under 25 were then saying they engaged in premarital sex. Moreover, 64% of women admit to at least one extra marital sex affair. Here in Canada, *The Toronto Star* puts it at 30% to 45%.

Consequently we read that V.D. has smitten ten million Americans and that there are more babies aborted than born to teenage mothers. The late Julian Huxley reckoned: man will eventually cure all destructive vice by psychological science. But Huxley is dead, and so is his theory. Oh, scientists are trying. But one year we read that people with XYZ chromosomes are dull and violent: potentially dangerous criminals; and the next year we're reading they're not! A few years ago we thought that the answer was psychiatry. But foremost North American psychiatrist Karl Menninger was quoted the other day: "I used to believe that psychiatry was the great hope for America. But now I feel it's failed, and I don't really know why. People in analysis don't really seem to get better, as I once hoped and thought they would."

What we need is not merely to pull the human race into a garage for an overhaul and a set of retreads. A pit stop is not enough. For his evil nature, man needs to be born again. Nothing less will do.

In 1976 I conducted a Crusade in Missouri, and I was asked to address a medical convention of 1200 physicians. I was sitting next to one of the doctors at breakfast. A devout Christian, he told me of a 29-year-old lady who had come to his clinic. She was rich. But she was crying. What had happened was that her husband had stepped out on her.

Enraged she resolved to get even. So she put on a mini and a plunging neckline sweater, and strutted out to a bar. She got a man all right. She also contracted a dirty disease. Yes, the doctor could cleanse it away with antibiotics. But the guilt, the dirty feeling she had—what was there for this? The kindly physician assured her: "The blood of Jesus Christ his Son cleanseth us from all sin" (1 John 1:7). Right there in the doctor's office she was born again in Christ, receiving His cleansing and salvation. Today she is the happy fulfilled and active member of a Christian church.

Here is a letter which came to our Agape office from Nova Scotia, which *Decision* magazine carried to its readers around the world:

> Over a year ago I asked Christ into my life. I was 26 years of age, single, and had a serious drinking problem. Physically I was torn apart. I had given up completely on everything and had nothing to live for. But one Sunday I turned on the Agape program—something I had never done in my life was to watch a program like that. Usually I'd switch the channel, but not that day; something told me not to. I was drinking at the time, but as I listened to the program Dr. White said that no matter what we had done or what our problem, there was hope and forgiveness in Jesus Christ. Right then it hit me so hard I threw away my drink and that was it. To me it was Jesus speaking, and from that day on my whole life has changed. I now have a purpose for living because of Jesus Christ and what he has done for me. Knowing that Jesus cares for those with problems like mine, I want to help them. What I heard on the program that day has brought me from death to life. I pray that many others will be helped by "Agape."

We need to be born again because *until we are, we are not complete persons.* Today we hear so much about the whole man, about the total woman, about the complete person. Ann Landers says she gets hundreds of letters from people who feel they are "worthless ... non-persons." Professor Chad Walsh writes in *Time* magazine that more than man wants bread when he's hungry, a beverage when he's thirsty, a bed when he's tired, or friends when he's lonely—yes, more than he wants romance or sex—he wants *atonement*. Atonement we get when we receive Christ. By Christ we "receive the atonement," wrote St. Paul to the Romans (8:10). And to the Colossians he wrote that when we have "received Christ Jesus the Lord" we are then, and not until then, "complete." In John 5 we read that Jesus stepped up to a man who had been chronically ill for 38 years and asked him: "Wilt thou be made whole?" (v. 6). The paralytic, whose inferiority complex had crippled his entire outlook on life, had begun to wallow in his inveterate self-pity and despair and to fall back on his longtime crutches. But Jesus was God. And He had impatience only with unbelief. When the man took Jesus seriously, he received the miracle of wholeness and followed Him. Two chapters later, when Christ's critics were crowding Him closely, our Lord simply pointed at this man and said: Here's my answer! Look! "I have made a man every whit whole." And that's the genius of Jesus. As God the Son, He makes people total! complete! whole! entire!

Has there ever been a time in human history when people wanted so much to be whole? The escalating lawsuits of uncured patients against the medical profession the last few years is surely evidence of this. People are desperate to be whole. Undoubtedly they expect too much from doctors. Medical men are not miracle workers. They never will be. Two million, two hundred thousand North

Americans see a medical doctor every day, 33 million going into hospitals every year. Last year 4.4 million sought psychiatric help, and 17 million had operations. Six percent of the physicians themselves are alcoholics, and the mental breakdowns and suicides among doctors are five times as high as among the rest of us. Toronto psychiatrist Dr. Roland Forrester said recently to the College of Family Physicians of Canada that medical costs are skyrocketing because people are turning more and more to doctors for their "sickness of the soul." This, in a day when abortively "the power of the church has moved to medicine."

Today peoples' incompleteness is chiefly that they are neglecting their souls. Foremost psychiatrist Victor Frankl reckons that his predecessor, Sigmund Freud, came saying; "Everyone knows he's got a soul; I'm going to show people they've got instincts." Today, states Frankl, all people know they've got instincts. Hugh Hefner has seen to that, but most people don't really know they've got souls! So they've left their lives bereft, incomplete, truncated.

Thank God that at least in North America there has been a return to a reemphasis on the soul as an essential ingredient of the human personality. Maple Leaf Gardens in Toronto recently welcomed Marvin Gaye for a Soul Concert. *The Vancouver Province* describes Ray Charles as "Packaged Soul." That's what all of us are. Jesus said your body is temporal—and at most not worth much. In today's economy, the body of man chemically is worth $5.60, as compared to 98 cents in 1936. No amount of inflation would bring the worth of your body up to the value of your soul. Jesus said it doesn't matter all that much if you lose your hand or foot. But don't sell your soul to hell, He said. Your soul, says Jesus, is indestructible and it is priceless! Actress Gloria Swanson says: "If you take care of your insides, the outside will take care of itself." I was walking through Hollywood and saw a sign: "Soul Unlimited Productions." If by unlimited, it is meant the soul's life is timelessly long, that's accurate. In Chicago, they originate the TV Soul Train. The real soul is a train that stretches across a measureless universe. Many a VIP is just a shell around an empty soul. "Jackie Onassis," writes Gail Harris in a Montreal magazine, "is a tortured soul." There is a cure for a tortured soul. It is to say a hearty yes to Jesus Christ, who fits into the soul like a hand into a glove.

I was conducting a crusade in Taegu, Korea, in 1973. On a Sunday afternoon many hundreds responded to open their lives to Christ. One was from the United States. He had wandered all his life in a vast wilderness of confusion—from university to university, from religion to religion, from country to country. That Sunday afternoon, he came forward to be born again in Christ. Previous to his new birth his mind would go one way, his conscience another direction, his feelings would be pulling another way and his will yet another. Now that he was born again in Christ, he had been synchronized in his soul and he found his mind, his conscience, his feelings and his will—all co-ordinated in Christ.

Then again, we need to be born again *because that's why Jesus Christ came into the world.* The word "must" is used twice in the third chapter of John. Jesus said to Nicodemus: "Ye *must* be born again" (v. 7), and in verse 14 we read: "As Moses lifted up the serpent in the wilderness, even so *must* the Son of man be lifted up." Jesus never demanded a response of man before imposing on Himself an infinitely greater commitment. Man's salvation was imperative, but impossible without Christ's sacrifice. Indeed, the very fact of Christ's death calls for us to be born again. "Forasmuch as ye know that ye were not redeemed with corruptible things, as silver and gold," wrote St. Peter, "but with the precious blood of Christ" (1 Pet. 1:18, 19). A pink diamond was sold in Zurich for a million and ninety-five thousand dollars. But that pink diamond was nothing compared to the priceless red drops of the blood of Jesus, shed for sinners. It is currently calculated that there are 9 trillion dollars worth of developed real estate in the world today. That's as nothing compared to the worth of the priceless blood of Jesus. His blood is worth more than the combined wealth of all of the material universes.

Joseph Stalin had on his desk—always—a globe of the world. From the dawn of creation God kept before Him a globe of this world. From all eternity "God so loved the world that he gave." Goethe, the German, once said: "If I were God, this world of sin and suffering would break my heart." Mr. Goethe, it did! Jesus, wrote the writer to the Hebrews, "suffered since the foundation of the world" in anticipation of the fact that he "appeared to put away sin by the sacrifice of himself" (Heb. 9:26).

The papers identified the biggest oak tree on earth the other day, in California. Not so big as the tree of Calvary! A bus recently knocked down the actual olive tree under which Plato taught 2,300 years ago; but it was as nothing compared to the tree on which the Son of God was cursed and crucified that we might be forgiven and forever His. Alexander Whyte, the Scot, was right to declare that Jesus Christ had one task in coming to earth: "Sin was

His errand in the world and it was His only errand. He would never have been in the world at all, but for sin." Your sin and my sin brought Him down to earth, then put Him up there on the cross.

In a Rocky Mountain community where I was holding a crusade in 1976, one morning at 7 a.m., I addressed two or three hundred society leaders. After shaking the guests' hands I stepped out to the street. There was a man, sitting in the cab of his pickup truck. Mike had heard me present Christ that morning, had gone home and come back! His only son, Mark, 20 years old, was to have played professional baseball for one of the major league teams that summer, but instead had been killed while up in the mountains on a fishing trip. Mike said: "My wife, Rose, and I cry all day—every day! But one thing: Before Mark was killed, he and I were in the meeting, and even though I didn't, he went forward and I know he's in heaven." Gripping his hand, I said: "Mike, God, too, had His only Son killed—on the cross for you!" Two nights later, Mike and Rose came forward to be born again, and a night or two after that, their only daughter, Debbie, and her boyfriend.

Finally, we must be born again, *because it is the difference between our going to heaven or to hell.* Jesus was explicit: "Except a man be born again, he can" neither "see the kingdom of God" (John 3:3) nor "enter into the kingdom of God" (v. 5). Among Jesus' last pronouncements on earth was His terribly solemn warning that while believers can be sure of salvation, "he that believeth not shall be damned" (Mark 16:16).

Dr. Kubler-Ross, the Swiss psychiatrist, currently believed to be the world's foremost expert on death, says after 30 years of clinical study: "It's not a matter of belief or opinion. I know beyond the shadow of a doubt that there is life after death." The current movie title is right: "You Only Live Twice"; or the TV program: "The Man Who Died Twice." The Bible speaks of "the second death" (Rev. 21:8) and of being "twice dead" (Jude 12). It teaches there's a life here and there's a life hereafter.

Of course people don't like to be reminded of death, but it's insane not to prepare for it. If you're a man, you've got a probable 71.4 life span; if you're a woman, 76. On the other hand, you're not assured of being alive for another minute. Recently, 55 relatives gathered to celebrate a man's birthday. When they arrived, instead, he died, and they had a funeral, not a celebration. In the comic strip "Dennis the Menace" the freckle-faced little guy was kneeling—but balking! He had reached the line in his bedtime prayer: "And if I should die before I wake...." Staring up over his shoulder he exclaimed: "Hey! I don't like that part!" Recently 33-year-old Julie Christie, star of "Darling," blurted out: "I'm desperately afraid—madly afraid—I can't stand the idea of growing old. I hate myself. I feel like crying. Perhaps it's because I have no religion to fall back on."

The Russians are digging a hole 50 miles deep, expecting to go through the earth's mantle to the brimstone core. Is that hell? I don't know. I do know the Bible says the way to stay out of hell is to be born again in Christ. I got a letter from a young person out West: "What's it like in hell?" I don't know anything beyond what the Bible says, because no one's ever come back to tell us. I saw a bumper sticker the other day: "Speed On, Brother. Hell Ain't Half Full." That, friend, is precisely why you should stop! Look! and Listen! Stop where you are. Look to Christ and listen to His Spirit calling you.

Bev Shea, Lowell Jackson and I were recently in a meeting in Kitchener, Ontario. At the end, Don Smith of Preston came up and told me that he had come into the Wesley United Church in Galt, 25 years before, and had come forward to be born again. During the intervening quarter of a century, he had grown in grace, had married a wonderful wife and they had four boys. I said, "Don, do you remember any special word that night which prompted you to come forward?"

He said, "Yes. It was when you said: 'I'd sooner be a foot out of hell and headed out, than a thousand miles out and headed in!' "

Martin Luther King, Sr., was on our Billy Graham Crusade platform in Atlanta a few years ago, and I remember what a fine man he was to talk to. Then the world was shocked one Sunday. His wife was shot right in his church, during a service, as he was preaching and she was sitting on the organ stool. As she went to be with Christ, Dr. King called after her "Bunch! Bunch! I'm coming on up home. I'll be home almost any time now!"

While I was writing this chapter, I went out to preach in East Toronto, and a middle-aged British lady named Nan came up to me afterwards. She had just come to Christ. But she had two sisters who had gone to the other world twenty or so years ago. Both, at the time, were in their thirties. Both had two children. Both were nominal Presbyterians. Sheila was 32. She had had a heart attack from which she was not to recover. I had gone around to her house and led her to Christ. From then until her death, a month later, she had been reading the Bible constantly, and telling everyone who came to see her about Christ. Then, one Sunday morning, while her family were en route to the local Presbyterian church, she had a final heart attack and went to heaven.

In contrast to this recollection, Nan had the haunting memory of her other sister Jean. Jean was 38 at the time. Depressed, dejected, with no apparent experience of Christ in her life, she had stuck her head in a gas oven and, insofar as Nan knew, gone to hell.

For twenty years this impression had followed Nan —around Britain and across the Atlantic, to her new home in Canada. Now she had finally settled it. She had been born again!

Chapter 3

What Being Born Again Is Not

Before we set out to establish from the Scriptures what it means to be born again, it is important that we point out what being born again is not. There are a great many misconceptions of what it means to be born again. If the devil cannot deter people from going to heaven, he will try very hard to deflect them into hell by deception.

To be born again is not *generation*. It is not something we can inherit or automatically acquire from our natural parents. They can lead us toward being born again by their prayers, their love, their example, their devotion to Christ, by their taking us regularly to where the Gospel is taught and proclaimed. And once we are born again, they can help nurture us in the Christian faith. But they cannot perform for us the act of being born again. A Canadian Catholic priest, Father Robert Mac-Dougal, puts it this way: "God has no spiritual grandchildren. Each person himself must be born again." In John 1:13 we read that to be born again is not to be born "of blood, nor of the will of the flesh, nor of the will of man, but of *God*." People can have the godliest of parents, but until they themselves have been born again, they're not Christians.

Bev Shea and I were in a beautiful new auditorium on the campus of the University of Brandon in Manitoba recently. Presiding over the gathering was the Reverend John Robb. He told of how, in Crossgar Presbyterian Church in Britain, where it was my privilege to be the evangelist 25 years ago, he had come forward to be born again at the age of 18. His father was a devout Anglican clergyman, a fervent evangelical. John had left home and bought a motorcycle. His employer had insisted on him attending that meeting. He had left early, and angrily roared off on his big bike. But the next night he was back, and came forward to be born again. He had since finished his academic and theological training, and had been pastoring churches in Eastern and Western Canada for 20 years, and in addition serving as religion editor and a radio and TV talk-show host.

Other people there are who associate being born again with *baptism*. Baptism is very important in the New Testament. But it does not ensure that its recipient is born again. We read in Acts 8 of Simon the Sorcerer of Samaria. When Philip the evangelist preached Jesus, many believed. Simon made his response and, we read, "was baptised." But when Peter arrived on the scene, he "perceived" Simon's "heart" was "not right in the sight of God"; that he was still "in the gall of bitterness, and in the bond of iniquity."

I received a letter from a lady in French Canada who had been baptized into the church as a child, but had no realization of spiritual fulfillment until one day she was watching our telecast and wrote, "On this day I have made a commitment to Jesus Christ our Saviour. I have been born again. He has healed me spiritually and I thank Him."

To be born again is not *confirmation.* I've heard people say that there is no mention of confirmation in the Bible. That is not so. What confirmation implies is, of course, differently interpreted by different denominations. In Acts 14 we read that Paul and Barnabas preached the Gospel and followed up by returning to where there were earlier converts "confirming the souls of the disciples, and exhorting them to continue in the faith" (v. 22). In chapter 15, we read of prophets Judas and Silas at Antioch exhorting the "brethren with many words and confirmed them" (v. 32). Later in the chapter we read how Paul and Silas retraced an earlier evangelistic itinerary through "Syria and Cilica, confirming the churches" (v. 41). Whatever the precise meaning of the word confirmation is, as implied by these verses, it is commonly agreed upon that confirmation into the membership of any visible church or denomination is not in itself being born again. Ideally it can be a sequel to being born again. Confirmation and being born again may take place at or about at the same time. But they are not synonymous.

I was conducting a crusade in Middle America one night when Judy, the 16-year-old daughter of the Lutheran minister there, came forward to receive Christ. Her father was the Chairman of the crusade. Baptized and confirmed, according to her own testimony, she had not yet been born again in Christ until that night. Her father told me later that she had written a very long letter addressed to "Dear God," a sentence of which reads: "I thank you, God, for sending your Son, Jesus, into my soul tonight to fill the empty place!" In another crusade in the Midwest the whole confirmation class of Holy Trinity Lutheran Church came forward to make decisions for Christ because, as their minister said, they wanted, like Martin Luther, to be sure that they were genuinely born again—not just confirmed into the church.

Nor is being born again *perspiration*. Too many people think that if they work hard enough at their religion, that ensures their being born again. St. Paul wrote to Titus (3:5) that it's "not by works of righteousness which we have done, but according to his mercy he saved us, by the washing of regeneration, and renewing of the Holy Spirit." To build a spiritual superstructure on a works foundation is perilous. We're not born again, as Martin Luther used to say, by faith *and* works, but by faith *that* works.

We were recently holding an Agape Rally in Windsor, Ontario, when a businessman named Herb came up and said: "May 24, 1970, was a beginning day for me. Though I was a Baptist deacon, my spiritual life was nil and my business was collapsing. I went to the hockey arena in Leamington, where you were holding a crusade. That night I gave my whole life to Christ. He not only met my spiritual need, but He also helped me, through a series of difficulties, to put my business together, and I've never looked back." He had previously done all the right things religiously, but it was not until he was born again in Christ that he experienced personal salvation.

Nor is to be born again *inspiration*: Jesus, in His parable of the sower, told of those who hear the Word of Life, but the seed has fallen into thin soil on a rock, and though the seedling germinates and the plant shoots up to meet the sun, it has shallow roots. So all too quickly it withers (Matt. 13). Many people get very inspired by religious rhetoric or aesthetic spiritual music or meditational techniques. But that is not being born again. To be born again is not a mere passing superficiality. It is a perennial reality with a beginning at a precise moment in time.

Early in 1976 I was in a crusade in the West. The caretaker of the beautiful auditorium was obliged to attend every night. For years he had heard some of the great American concert hall presentations and had been greatly inspired on occasion. One night in the crusade, he came forward to be born again. His name was Dick Null, and laughingly he said to me afterwards: "My name's Null. Until tonight, my life was *null!*—and void. Now I'm Christ's."

Nor is to be born again *education*. St. Paul wrote to Timothy about those who are "ever learning, and never able to come to the knowledge of the truth" (2 Tim. 3:7). The only apostle who had the advantages of a first-class education was St. Paul. He warned of those whose "trust" (really) is undermined by "profane and vain babblings, and oppositions of science falsely so called" (1 Tim. 6:20). Paul vividly recalled when he had preached Christ in the Athenian Aereopagus and leading the opposition to being born again were "certain philosophers of the Epicureans and of the Stoicks" (Acts 17:18). So he wrote to the Colossians (2:8) that they should "beware lest any man spoil you through philosophy and vain deceit." It was, of course, not acquiring true knowledge that St. Paul warned them against. It was, as he wrote to the Corinthians, when "knowledge puffeth up" (2 Cor. 8:1) and thrusts out the true knowledge of God. Jesus in fact is the True "Key to knowledge."

The 20th century has certainly been one in which hundreds of millions of people have felt that education was validly above any form of religion. As recently as in the mid sixties, the Hall-Dennis Report was headily assuring Canadians, that insofar as academic learning was concerned we could rest assured that: "Education is the instrument which will break the shackles of ignorance, of doubt, and of frustration; that will take all who respond to its call out of their poverty, their slums and their despair; that will give mobility to the crippled; that will illuminate the dark world of the blind; that will carry solace to the disordered of mind, imagery to the slow of wit, and peace to the emotionally disturbed": All of these achievements, allegedly, without any allusion whatsoever to peoples' hearts being changed by Jesus Christ.

Did this euphoric dream find fulfillment in Canada, the United States—or anywhere? Of course not. Jesus said: "Without me, ye can do nothing" (John 15:5). Recently a University of Toronto President John Evans lamented: "Until a few years ago it was commonly accepted by academics that through research most of the major problems of society could be solved." Gradually, however, we came to realize "that most of these problems weren't solved . . . they were still there. And in fact they were getting bigger." The current philosophical crisis in education can be seen in the frame of mind of the Canadian people. While 84% are satisfied with the policing of this country, and even 81% with the Post Office, only 42% are happy about the educational state of affairs. University of Toronto Professor James Eayrs reckons: "There is a malaise abroad in the academy, a sickness of the spirit." How true that observation is: which brings us back to Jesus' insistence to Nicodemus that he "must be born again."

One of the world's foremost mathematical brains of our times is the Russian, Dr. Boris Dotsenko, now at the University of Toronto. He was brought up as an atheist in Marxism, but in working through some profound technical aspects of the 4th Law of Thermo

Dynamics in higher physics, he became convinced
(as is the case with thousands of scientists today)
that there had to be a God. On a science assignment
to Canada, he opened up a Gideon Bible in his hotel
room, and Who walked out of its pages, right into
his heart, but Jesus Christ. Seeking and getting asy-
lum, he is today a fascinating testifier to the reality
of being born again.

There are those who mistake *renunciation* for being born again. Annually during lent many people
will deny themselves luxuries and pleasures which
the rest of the year they will indulge as if they were
going out of style. There is no doubt but what self-
denial is a major part of Christian discipline. But,
D. L. Moody used to say, "we don't work toward
the cross, but from the cross." *The Toronto Globe
and Mail* recently asked; "How is it that we need
millions of laws to enforce Ten Commandments?"
Actually St. Paul declared: "The law of the spirit
of life in Christ Jesus hath made me free from the
law of sin and death" (Rom. 8:2). Our Lord gave us
that remarkable parable of the Pharisee and the Publican. The Pharisee paraded brazenly before an on-
looking public gallery, that he was no extortioner
or adulterer. He wasn't unjust. He fasted not merely
once, but twice a week. He gave tithes. In contrast,
beside him was a publican whose capacity for renunciation or abstinence from evil habit of any kind was
nearly nill. So he simply fell to his face in prayer
and invoked: "God be merciful to me a sinner!" (Luke
18:9-14). And Jesus said that that man went down
to his house justified. He had been born again, not
by renunciation, but by a request for mercy and the
acceptance of Christ's grace.

In a crusade in San Bernardino, California, in
1976, a lovely lady by the name of Jackie came for-

ward one night and later told me that that was the occasion of her being born again. She had been such a devout church-goer that often she went daily to seek absolution for her sins. But somehow she had never placed her guilt squarely and fully on Jesus, and received His forgiveness and assurance of everlasting salvation. That night she did.

Some think *reformation* is what it means to be born again. One who followed Jesus for three years, and who outwardly conformed but was never inwardly regenerated, was Judas. Because he had never really followed Jesus, when the real crunch came, he betrayed Him. The multitudes probably never gave a second thought as to whether or not he was a true disciple. They took for granted that he was. Only Jesus and Judas himself knew that however reformed outwardly he appeared, inwardly, as Jesus put it, he was a devil. George Bernard Shaw made the ridiculous observation: "Anyone who would reform himself, must first of all reform society." Actually that is why the world is in such a mess today: do-gooders trying to heal mankind's cancer by attacking his skin rashes, rather than going to the vital organs; secular humanists attempting to reform society from the outside in, rather than from the inside out. "Can We Reform Criminals by Forced Medical Therapy?" asks the headlines of a metropolitan daily! "No!" is the reply, in a discussion which has had a lot of ink in North America recently. We need the transforming power of Jesus Christ. Will Durant notes: "Caesar hoped to reform men by changing institutions and laws; Christ wished to remake institutions and lessen laws by changing men." I saw another recent headline which complained: "Alcohol Problem Has No Solution!" Yes, it does! Jesus Christ assured us that if we are born again, He undertakes not only to forgive our sins but also to deliver us from their power.

Many mistake *imitation* for being born again. They will say something like this: "Doesn't the Bible state: "Be ye followers of God?" Yes, it does, but that first verse of Ephesians 4, quoted in full, exhorts: "Be ye therefore followers of God, as dear children." The key is "dear children." Jesus stated to Nicodemus, a Pharisee, that to become God's children, men need to be born again; for all men, including unregenerated Pharisees, were of their "father the devil" (John 8:44).

Charles Sheldon's *In His Steps* was a book written two generations ago, which became one of this century's best sellers. It was based on the exhortation of Peter that believers in Christ "should follow His steps" (1 Pet. 2:21). Millions tried to be Christlike without being Christ's. It has proven as impossible as it would be for an unborn baby to walk and talk like his father. He has to be born before he can even begin on that track. In John 1:12 we read: "But as many as received him, to them gave he power to become the sons of God, even to them that believe on his name." So reception of Christ into our hearts must precede any serious effort on our part to live like Him in our conduct. I recall the night in 1969 in South Dakota when a lad came forward to be born again. Later he described the change: "I feel my heart so big that Jesus not only moved in himself, but He moved in all His furniture." His imitation of Christ was energized by the awareness that Christ had taken up residence in his life.

Some mistake *co-operation* for being born again. This is nearly as old a notion as the human race itself. Back at Babel, men decided that rather than God coming down to man in his need, men should meet God halfway. So co-operation took over. And we read that the people of the Shinar Peninsula set about to build an ideal city, and in the center of it a tower of burnt brick which would reach up into heaven.

What followed is literary history. We read, "And the Lord came down to see the city and the tower, which the children of men builded. And the Lord said, Behold, the people is one, and they have all one language; and this they begin to do; and now nothing will be restrained from them, which they have imagined to do. Go to, let us go down, and there confound their language, that they may not understand one another's speech. So the Lord scattered them abroad from thence upon the face of all the earth; and they left off to build the city" (Gen. 11:5-9). Some of the places they went to, as recorded in that chapter, have turned up in the amazing 15,000 scrolls in Syria two Jesuit archeologists from Rome recently excavated and unearthed.

The upshot is that man went from one language to the 3,000 he speaks in today. Why? Because the Kingdom of God is not entered by the door of humanism. Marx's co-operative ventures—the League of Nations, the U.S., all built on secular humanism —have aborted. Man is made for God. Only God can make him work individually or corporately.

Oddly enough this language problem is what is currently threatening to split Canada into two countries. It's ironic that history repeats itself. To try and spread around the spirit of co-operation, while I am writing, headlines announce that here in Toronto, from atop the world's tallest tower, they're planning to transmit in 18 languages from a new TV station. Man is extremely proud, and therefore extremely reluctant to come to terms with the fact that his vertical relationship with God is paramount. And only from such a vertical relationship can a horizontal relationship of loving his brothers and sisters spring.

While I was writing this chapter, I found that I was using a pen which was given to me by a very distinguished man. He had been a Senator. He had owned and published a newspaper. He had a summer home near where I was holding a crusade in the Midwest. A devout church member, he was not sure of ever having really been born again. So this night he and his wife both came forward to confess Jesus Christ as their Lord and Saviour.

There are many people who stumble over the misconception that to be born again is *aspiration*. The rich young ruler aspired to eternal life, but he went back to his riches rather than wholly follow Jesus. The prophet/philosopher Baalam took a look at ancient Israel and aspired: "Let me die the death of the righteous, and let my last end be like his!" (Num. 23:10). But Jude said he hankered even more for the wages of unrighteousness, and so went out through the doors of death into the darkness of doom. Baalam and the rich young ruler preferred to continue undisturbed in their life-style, as sophisticated drifters.

Finally, it is important to clarify that to be born again is not *inclination*. There are many people who go far beyond aspiration and almost decide for the Lord, but somehow don't quite cross over the bridge. "Almost thou persuadest me to be a Christian," exclaimed King Agrippa from his throne to prisoner Paul, only to receive the urgent entreaty to move from the tragic quagmire of "almost" to being "altogether" a Christian (Acts 26:28, 29).

In the mid-sixties I was preaching in a stadium in western Canada. The chairman of that crusade was a medical doctor. On a Saturday, a Presbyterian minister felt an undeniable urge to get a man called George into the crusade meeting. That night he had him in for supper and George, not without reluctance, came along. I preached Jesus' words, "This night thy soul shall be required of thee." George heard an inner voice say, "This is the way, walk ye in it." There was a fierce spiritual battle going on in his will. But eventually, he broke loose from the devil's hold and from high in the stands, he made his way forward, where he prayed the prayer of decision for Christ that he might be born again. Sooner than for most, Jesus called: "This night thy soul shall be required of thee" to George. That very night, in fact, he was alone in his home. The gas main broke and his house blew up. Rushed to the hospital with third-degree burns, he had standing over him the physician who was the Crusade Chairman—and the Presbyterian minister. George apparently regained consciousness only once before he took his flight to his long home. The beloved physician heard him mutter almost inaudibly, "Doc, I'm glad I did it! I gave myself to Jesus." And born again as he was, he went to be with Christ.

Chapter 4

What It Is To Be Born Again

Since Jesus insisted we *must* be born again, and we've just looked at common misconceptions of what it means to be born again, it is imperative that we turn and look at the positive side: "What it is to be born again." Jimmy Carter was elected President of the United States on the slogan: "A Leader for a Change." That's what Jesus Christ is: the Lord of change. One of the most read books today is Ullmann's *Changing*. People know they need to be changed. Being born again is a change: we change our minds and Christ changes our hearts. "Look," wrote W. H. Auden centuries ago, "for a change of heart." It's a basic life quest.

Alexander Solzhenitsyn in *Gulag II* observed: "It gradually became clear to me, that the line dividing good and evil does not run between states, classes or parties. It runs through every human heart." Solomon the wise instructed his sons: "Keep thy heart with all diligence; for out of it are the issues of life" (Prov. 4:23). Sir Walter Raleigh, when about to be beheaded, remarked to his executioner in his famous last words: "So the heart be right, it is no matter which way the head lieth." For centuries the arguments have gone on as to whether man's head or heart rules his will. Eleanor Roosevelt asked the philosopher to Presidents, Bernard Baruch, which, when there seemed to be conflict between her head and her heart, she should follow. "Follow your heart," counselled Baruch. Pascal perhaps put it most rationally when he reckoned, "The heart has its reasons which are quite unknown to the head."

But here we can run into trouble. Physically heart trouble is the number one killer. And spiritually, heart trouble is man's lethal destroyer. Noted a socialist Prime Minister of Britain: "Our real problem is not the H bomb, but the human heart." Much of the thought life of the 20th century, of course, has been dominated by a humanism which contended that the human heart is intrinsically good. That theory is dying hard today, but it is dying. The eminent columnist Robert Fulford notes that unlike our fathers, we're shut up to the realization that "people aren't good at heart and that's the aching truth."

Turning to the Bible, Jesus taught plainly that "from within, out of the heart of men, proceed evil thoughts, adulteries, fornications, murders, thefts, coveteousness, wickedness, deceit, lasciviousness, an evil eye, blasphemy, pride, foolishness: all these evil things come from within, and defile the man" (Mark 7:21-23). Simon Peter diagnosed Simon the sorcerer: "Thy heart is not right in the sight of God" (Acts 8:21). Jeremiah (17:9) could scarcely have been stronger: "The heart is deceitful above all things, and desperately wicked: who can know it?" Nor has this been a gradual deterioration in the innate state of the human heart. In the beginning of history, prior to Noah's coming on the scene, we read that "God saw the wickedness of man was great in the earth, and that every imagination of the thoughts of his heart was only evil continually" (Gen. 6:5).

So with man's heart that bad, it needs renewal. "I will take the stony heart out," promised God to Ezekiel, and "I will put a new spirit within you" (Ezek. 11:19). For a person to receive a new heart, it often takes a broken heart: "A broken and a contrite heart," the Lord has promised not to ignore (Ps. 51:17). This can lead to an open heart. In Acts 16:14, we read of Lydia "whose heart the Lord opened." When Christ enters your heart, He will "create" within "a clean heart" (Ps. 51:10).

One Sunday afternoon on Agape when I prayed with those who wished to give their hearts to Christ, a Nova Scotian writes: "I gave my heart to the Lord. What an experience. Jesus said if you're burdened, just take it to Him in prayer. It's wonderful and I wouldn't be without Jesus for anything. I have never been happier in my whole life." In Proverbs 16:20, we read: "Whoso trusteth in the Lord, happy is he."

To be born again is not only a change of heart but a change of mind. Habakkuk (1:11) wrote that a man can undergo a "mind change." When the maniac of Gadara met Christ, one of the wildest men in the Bible was changed into a man: "in his right mind" (Mark 5:15).

You see, inherently man's "mind is enmity against God" (Rom. 8:7), so that we were born "alienated, enemies" to Him in our "mind" (Col. 1:21), and the result is that the "mind" of universal man instinctively "is defiled": Christless people become "men of corrupt minds" (2 Tim. 3:8). Who did it? Satan! St. Paul wrote that "the god of this world hath blinded the minds of them which believe not" (2 Cor. 4:4).

Twenty years ago in Britain the most quoted psychiatrist was Londoner Dr. William Sargeant whose book *Battle for the Mind* has become a classic.

nt resurfaced in the mid-seventies in connec-
....th Patty Hearst's trial. After five sessions with
Miss Hearst he was convinced that her being violently
seized, gagged, hit over the head and blindfolded in
a closet for 60 days had the effect of her being mentally altered—brainwashed (to use a term which de-
rives from the modern Chinese). The Bible tells us
that the devil blinds human minds, then he brain-
washes, and takes possession of them.

But by the same token, when we become Christ's,
He changes our minds by possessing them. St.
Paul wrote to the Philippians (2:5): "Let this mind
be in you, which was also in Christ Jesus." You actually can "have the mind of Christ" (Phil. 2:16).
So you're "transformed by the renewing of your
minds" (Rom. 12:2). Those of us who are Christians
can be assured that "God hath given us . . . a sound
mind."

If while I was at Oxford in the late fifties I
had been asked to name the ablest literary figure
on the international scene, I would have said,
Malcolm Muggeridge, then editor of *Punch* and Rector of the University of Edinburgh. He was an ag-
nostic. Then, in the sixties, he was born again, and
is known today throughout the world as a man with
a mind totally dedicated to Christ. One of his stunned,
highly intellectual relatives, now of Toronto, wrote
in Canada's leading news magainze, *McLeans*, under the byline: "Confession of Faith in Christ" that
Muggeridge right at the "height of his popularity and
universal acceptance as the western world's official
iconoclast . . . suddenly declared that he had found
Christ. He told the world that Jesus was his Saviour. He had met Him—just as the two had on
the Emmaus road, walking northwest from Jerusalem." Muggeridge wrote about it in his book: *Jesus Rediscovered.*

What is it to be born again? It is a change of conscience. The unregenerate man has a "weak" conscience (1 Cor. 8:10), a "defiled" conscience (Titus 1:15); a "dead" conscience (Heb. 9:14). Ann Landers published a letter recently from a young man who was so deeply anxious about his "conscience" that he "contemplated suicide"—this because "the other day at school (I'm a junior, age 16) I wanted to shoot a kid in my class. I actually wanted to kill him. If I had had a gun I could have shot everybody in the class and felt no more emotion than if I had trimmed a toenail." Psychiatrist Karl Menninger writes a book on *Whatever Happened to Sin?* in which he wonders what has happened to the conscience of modern man. Is it dead?

When we're born again, our conscience is brought alive in Christ. The writer to the Hebrews (9:14) put it: "How much more shall the blood of Christ, who through the eternal spirit offered himself without spot to God, purge your conscience from dead works to serve the living God?" The outcome is that the believer in Christ will have an affinity with Paul who declared: "I exercise myself, to have always a conscience void of offence toward God and toward man." President Garfield was converted to Christ as a teenager, and one day, as President of the United States he was asked privately to do something that looked extremely attractive, if very wrong, it being urged upon him: "Nobody will know!" "President Garfield will know, and I've got to sleep with him!" replied the President. Pat Boone, a believer in Christ, was asked on a talk show why he had that clean look. "A clear conscience," was his reply.

I recently received a letter from Walter Allen in the British Isles. It was concerning Tommy Brown, who prior to July, 1956, hadn't been to church since he had been in the Royal Air Force 20 years prior. He was a compulsive gambler and a chronic alcoholic and he seemed to have no conscience whatsoever about not providing for his family or doing anything useful with his life. One night he came to a crusade I was holding in Port Rush. He went home without making a decision. At midnight he went outside and walking up and down convicted in his conscience, he felt he'd die if he didn't do something about it. Finally, he knelt down in the grass, in a gentle rain, and on the basis of Romans 10:13, "Whosoever shall call upon the name of the Lord shall be saved," was born again in Christ. He was rid immediately and completely of his alcoholism and gambling craze. And now with a cleansed conscience, he became the kind of husband and father to their three children which has made it possible for them to be a fulfilled family in the worship and service of Christ.

What is it to be born again? It is a change of feeling. It is not an exaggeration to say that most people today fight a losing battle with their feelings. When I was at the Montreal Olympics, two peerless celebrities were quoted. Number one football superstar O. J. Simpson said he wanted to get out of athletics, into acting. That same day superstar Peter Sellers, the actor, lamented ironically enough that he wished he could be a star athlete, not an actor. He reflected: "The realization is less than the expectation. I tell you straight. All I am trying to do is get through the day. And when I cry, I cry for yesterday." Frank Sinatra says he drinks Jack Daniels whiskey just to get through the night.

The eminent Dr. Ian Henderson, Chairman of the Canadian Medical Association, says that currently one in five women insist on being within reach of a tranquilizer—to stave off depression. Strong addictional drugs such as valium are becoming more and more in demand—not always legally procured. Hard drug usage among women has increased 24% in two years.

It is far too widely assumed, however, that being born again is merely emotionalism. Emotional fulfillment is only one of the many by-products of a continuing experience of Christ. Sigmund Freud, in his *The Future of An Illusion*, reckoned: "Religion is the universal, compulsive neurosis of mankind." "Religion" may be a neurosis, but truly being born again in Christ is not. It is both intimate and ultimate reality. Freud's Vienese successor, Dr. Victor Frankl, states, "There is . . . a religious sense deeply rooted in each and every man's unconscious depths."

All men are born, feeling within them, though they can't articulate it, that they need to be born again. Having said that, it is important to note that it is very dangerous for us to put trust in feelings as a basis for salvation. Feelings are themselves a very poor barometer in the storms of life. Feeling is not a word used often in the Bible—under a dozen times, in fact. It's first usage was when Rebecca and Jacob teamed up to procure a blessing from the blind and aged Isaac by Jacob's putting on fur gloves so that Isaac thought he was Esau (Gen. 27:12). St. Paul, on the other hand addressing the erudite Athenians, declared that all peoples "seek the Lord" and "feel after him" (Acts 17:26, 27)—usually, however, without the willingness to repent. In Ephesians (4:18, 19) he explained that more often than not, people "because of the blindness of their heart" are actually "past feeling" and therefore miss knowing God because they've "given themselves over unto lasciviousness, to work all uncleanness." For those of us who do become Christ's, "we have not an high priest which cannot be touched with the feeling of our infirmities" so "let us therefore come boldly unto the throne of grace that we may obtain mercy, and find grace to help in time of need" (Heb. 4:15, 16).

While I was writing this chapter, I had handed to me the *Houston Post*, in which appeared the initial testimony of George Foreman, thought by many to be the world's strongest heavyweight boxer of the 1970's. He was the world champion in 1973, 74. At this moment, his profession of conversion is only a month old, and the inclusion of his words here are simply an expression of how it feels for some people when they are born again. Foreman, in describing himself as a "born-again Christian," exults: "All I can say is that I am now the happiest man in the world. I can't explain it. No one would understand it. I have found the truth. I am like a little child."

His becoming a "born-again Christian" took place immediately after his upset defeat by Jimmy Young in Puerto Rico, nullifying a 15 million dollar return fight with Mohammed Ali. At first, as he left the ring and entered his dressing room he was understandably traumatically disappointed, bitter, and nearly inconsolable: but not quite. As he sat there alone, suddenly, he says, "I felt my head, and when I brought my hands down, I saw there was blood on the palms of both hands. Then I looked down and saw there was blood on my feet. I was reminded that there was where Jesus bled—on His palms, on His feet and on His head. At that moment, I died. I died for God. Then I got life as a new creature. I became like a small, trusting baby. I had never read the Bible before. Now I read it all the time. I understand it. I want to explain to other people so that they, like me, can know the truth."

What was he doing a month after his born again Christian experience? His reply: "I go from California to New York to Florida to Texas. I travel alone. I travel with a Bible in my brief case. I don't want to go to big churches. I am not looking for fame or publicity. I don't want to sell any more washing powder and razor blades on television. I don't want to make headlines—I just want to talk to the plain people. I just want to go around the country, telling people what happened to me so it could happen to them." You could hardly say that being born again has not had a deep effect on George Foreman's feelings.

Our next point, being born again in Christ is a change of appetite, could scarcely be more aptly illustrated than in the testimony of George Foreman. Spiritual "new born babes desire" (1 Pet. 2:2) noted St. Peter. They desire to "walk in newness of life" (Rom 6:4). They desire to "serve in newness of spirit" (Rom. 7:6). They desire to sing "a new song" (Rev. 5:9). They desire to abide by "a new commandment"—love (2 John 5)—all because, and St. Paul did not state that there were exceptions, "if any man be in Christ, he is a new creation: old things are passed away; behold, all things are become new" (2 Cor. 5:17).

Sometimes I watch some of those television ads and wonder if they were written by someone trying to counterfeit a spiritual experience of Christ. For instance, in my thinking it's not Datsun who really best can say "Let the Spirit move you!" It's Jesus. And it's Jesus, not Volkswagen Rabbit, who can really claim "Happy days are here again!" It's Jesus, not Volvo, who is really "For the people who think!" It's Jesus, not Dainty Bol, who really "Makes the clean choice!" It's Jesus, not Fab, who really "Gets it deep down clean!" It's Jesus, not Chanel No. 5, who really "Puts it all together!" It's Jesus, not Right Guard, who's really "Double protection!" It's Jesus, not 7-UP, where "There's nothing like it so come on over."

How being born again can change a person's appetite was demonstrated in the life of a man who came forward to give his life to Christ in a California crusade I conducted in the mid-seventies. He, as head of the Rotary Club, presided over a united service club gathering I addressed one midday. That night he came to the crusade, and at the end came forward to be born again in Christ. His appetite for years had been a vulturous and voluptuous search for pornographic magazines. He had 300 pounds of them in his house at the time. It was not only a menace to him, but a very sore point with his family. That night, going home from the crusade he put all those magazines in the garbage, and with a new heart and mind, he could thereafter give himself fully to Christ as a son, to his family as a wholesome husband and father, and to his society as a contributing public servant.

Finally to the question: "What is it to be born again?" It is a change of the will. "If there be first a willing mind," wrote St. Paul, "it is accepted according to that a man hath, and not according to that he hath not" (2 Cor. 8:12). There is nearly no area of the human personality which struggles more with confronting change than the will. "Fear of change perplexes Monarchs," wrote John Milton 300 years ago; and his contemporary, Richard Hooker, noted: "Change is not made without inconvenience, even from worse to better." A hundred years prior, Michel DeMontaingne was even more emphatic, calculating that there seemed to be among humans "no state so bad... that it is not preferable to change."

On the other hand, it is imperative, that if anyone is to respond to God's call to be born again, that person must say "I will" to Christ. To Nicodemus, Jesus avowed that be it he or anyone else in the world, being born again swung on the response "that whosoever believeth in him, should not perish, but have everlasting life." Henry Ward Beecher once declared that there were only two classes of people in the world: the "whosoever wills" and the "whosoever won'ts": the "saints" and the "aints." Immanuel Kant, the philosopher, once declared that the only really good thing in man was the good will: until that, nothing.

Because of the stubbornness of man's will, God, to assert His will, sometimes uses the trial of tragedy to get people to a triumphant resignation of their will to Christ. Joe was a star athlete as a high schooler in a small town, pitching for the baseball team, quarterbacking the football team, and centering the basketball team. In University he was a letterman in sports, and while studying law he fell in love with the campus queen. She was a Christian and reluctant to be his bride until he said yes to Christ. But he courted her, and, yes, she married him at graduation. A lawyer, brilliant, he went far, fast, and within six or eight years was running for high stakes in politics.

But cancer hits one home in three and the former campus queen was an early victim. A wonderful Christian, before she passed she implored: "Joe, please promise to become a Christian and bring our little girl to heaven with you!" Then she passed away. Some broken hearts weep. Others can't cry and that's worse. Joe could shed no tears. The funeral was huge, and the minister, a presenter of Christ. It was deep in December when the shadows gather early. When Joe and the flaxen-haired wee girl went home that night, he put her to bed, and then headed in alone. Hardly into his room he heard her voice: "Daddy, are you there?"

"Yes! Darling, Daddy's here!"

"Daddy, can you love through the dark?"

"Yes, darling, Daddy can love through the dark!"

"Daddy, would you come and take me up in your big strong arms and tell me I'm your very own?"

"Yes, darling!" and he did!

And that was the longest night Joe had ever known. The wedding gift clock chimed out the whiling hours, and Joe rolled between the linens, with each strike launching a new hour of painful memories come to torture him in his neglect of Christ. There was his childhood when he had said no to Jesus in Sunday school, then church when the entreaties of his pastor went unheeded. Then there was the University Chapel where the college minister never failed to make plain a student's need to be born again. And most recently in his attendances at church with his devout wife when never a service went by but what he knew she was hoping this would be the time. But Jesus had never really left him alone. So finally, at the darkest hour of the night, just before the dawn, Joe slipped out beside his bed and looking up asked: "Jesus, are you there?"

The Light of the world flashed back, "Yes, Joe, I'm here!"

"Jesus, can you love through the dark?"

And the still small Voice signalled: "Yes, Joe."

And Joe said: "Jesus, can you come and take me up into your big strong arms and tell me I'm your very own?" And with that, the darkness turned to dawn. The Eternal Christ became Joe's Refuge, and underneath, the Everlasting Arms. He had been born again, and would soon become one of the great preachers of his day.

Chapter 5

Who Can Be Born Again?

When the rich young ruler came to Jesus and asked: "Good Master, what shall I do to inherit eternal life?" (Luke 18:18), our Lord made the demands of Christian discipleship very severe. Perhaps He envisaged this man as one of His premier apostles. I do not know. In any event, Jesus insisted that he should go and dispose of all his possessions and then come and follow Him. The rich young ruler balked at this and went sadly away. Jesus' disciples were amazed and asked: "Who then can be saved?" (v. 26). Jesus explained that being saved, being born again, was a miracle—never less! "The things which are impossible with men are possible with God."

In contrast, as if to make the point more emphatic, Jesus had just been dealing with the matter of children being born *again*. It is not insignificant that it was into this theme that the rich young ruler broke and came forward to Jesus, who was dealing with those who had "brought unto him, also infants, that he would touch them: but when his disciples saw it, they rebuked them. But Jesus called them unto him, and said, Suffer little children to come unto me, and forbid them not: for of such is the kingdom of God. Verily I say unto you, Whosoever shall not receive the kingdom of God as a little child shall in no wise enter therein" (Luke 18:15-17).

When I was a child in Saskatchewan the Sheppards lived on the next farm. Arthur and I were born a few weeks apart in 1928. In 1929 the depression struck, and with it the decade of drought. The Sheppard house burned down and finally Mr. Sheppard died from cancer. In 1934 Arthur and I started to school and we were the sole members of the grade I class in a ten-grade schoolroom.

A spiritual revival had moved through our community. All the Sheppards and Whites, except Arthur, were born again. One day Mrs. Sheppard and Arthur, aged seven, were out in the yard and the hen under the coop clucked, calling in her chickens. Mrs. Sheppard was singing: "When the roll is called up yonder, I'll be there." Arthur asked her what it meant. She explained: "Jesus is coming. And like at school, He has a roll call, and if your name is written on that roll, you'll go, and if it's not, you won't."

Within minutes Mrs. Sheppard tipped over an apple box, which had been used as a chair, and Arthur asked Jesus to come into his life, so that when the roll was called up yonder he'd be there. And there's no one in Canada today I'd sooner hear preach the Gospel than my lifetime friend and longtime pastor of the Evangelistic Tabernacle in Vancouver, the Rev. Arthur E. Sheppard.

It is precisely because Jesus insisted that all who enter His kingdom must have a childlike (not childish) faith, and because people like Arthur Sheppard and I came initially to Jesus as small children, that I always rejoice when I see or hear of children coming to Christ. I am writing this chapter in Riverside, California, where Dick Caddock lives. He told me at lunch that back in the sixties, his boy Jimmy, then five, shocked his parents by insisting on coming forward in one of our crusades here in Southern California. In retrospect, Dick reckons Jimmy was as distinctively born again as Saul of Tarsus was on the Damascus Road.

On the other hand, there is nothing to prevent people in their prime from being born again, except their own reluctance to respond to Christ's call. Paul the apostle was such a person. He had regrets that his conversion was not until he was in midstream.

Sometimes, insofar as reason is involved in the process of conversion, when a person in his prime sees the futility of lives around him being wasted without Christ, this in itself is a powerful incentive to respond to the call of Christ.

Attorney and Federal Commissioner Judge Roger Gay, perhaps 50 years old, came forward in a crusade I conducted in the early seventies. He had been handing down sentences for many years. He had two hangups: the recidivism of the people he sentenced and his own empty life. He asked Jesus Christ to come into his life, cleanse him from his sin, and testified that he now knew he was born again.

A short time ago I was standing in the doorway of our crusade site a moment, and a Christian youth worker came up to me. He was eager to tell me that his survey had revealed that only one in 1,100 who comes to Christ does so after the age of 70. It so happened that the previous night two senior ladies had come to our crusade, neither of whom had assurance from the Holy Spirit that they had ever been born again. One of them had a heart attack in the doorway of the crusade building. The other came forward to put her faith in Christ.

In the Scriptures there were those who, for differing reasons, did not meet Christ until they were senior citizens. In the second chapter of Luke, we read of an elderly man, Simeon, who had waited all his life for the coming of Christ. When he finally met Christ, he declared that he was, at last, ready to die. Then there was Anna. She experienced her moment of truth with Christ the Lord when she was 84 years of age.

Earlier in the seventies, I held two summer crusades. In one of them Harry Laughlin, a lifelong Baptist, came forward to be born again. He was 86. He told me that many times throughout his life, he had come close to the door of decision for Christ and then had backed off. In the second crusade 96-year-old Thomas Hudson finally responded one night to the call of Christ.

People of all ages do come to Christ. But, the earlier one does so, the better.

Who can be born again? Those at the bottom of society. In Luke 7, we read the account of Jesus going to eat in the house of Simon, a prominent Pharisee. Up to Him came a woman who apparently was a prostitute, fell to her knees, washed His feet with her tears, dried them with her hair, poured precious ointment on them and implored Jesus' forgiveness and cleansing from all her sins.

In the mid-seventies, I was conducting a crusade in a huge high school facility in Indianapolis when a lovely young lady came to give her testimony. Strangely enough she neither knew her own real name nor her birthday, but she was renamed Cornelius St. John by the Teen Challenge Center where she now lives, loves and serves; and a test of her bone marrow indicated she was about 16. She was apparently born to an alcoholic prostitute in Toronto. She was sent off for adoption, but it didn't work out.

She ran away to the United States and bounced from foster home to foster home. Finally, she sank down into the drug culture and went on heroin. To support her habit, she masterminded and pulled off a $150,000 robbery. The long arm of the law caught her and imprisoned her, but she broke out. It was while she was on the run that a Christian family picked her up as she was hitchhiking down the highway. They gave her the first love she ever really had, and with legal help, got her into their custody. Then they led her to Christ, who changed her from the inside out. Today, you'd never believe that Cornelius St. John was ever anything but a princess in the Kingdom of Christ. There may have been questions about her first birth, but there certainly weren't any about her second birth.

Many of us saw in the papers the story of Clyde Thompson. His own words were: "I was a bitter and angry man. I killed four men, and if I'd had the opportunity, I would have killed more. But toward the end of my 28 years and two months behind bars, a miracle happened. I began to read the Bible and experience God's love. I gave up fighting the system and turned my life over to Christ. When I was released from prison in 1955, I entered the Lord's work full time as a minister." For twenty years he has been a faithful preacher of the Gospel.

Who can be born again? Those in the upper echelons of society! Queen Victoria had a wonderful awakening to the call of Christ, and kept alert to the Holy Spirit's guidance throughout her life. One Sunday she heard her Canon speak from First Corinthians. There is a passage in the first chapter which says: "Ye see your calling, brethren, how that not many wise men after the flesh, not many mighty, not many noble are called." Queen Victoria asserted that she had been saved by one letter: the letter "m"; "not *m*any noble" she exulted; "St. Paul didn't say "not any," but "not *m*any."

In mid 1976, I held a crusade in a stadium in Texas where an orthopedic surgeon, Dr. Andrew Bahm, came forward to be born again. He was making $120,000 a year at the time, but had no peace. His wife had dragged him to the meeting. He'd tried everything within reach, but had gone round and round seeking fulfillment as a workaholic, as a playboy, and as a culture vulture. But he'd missed the most intimate and ultimate dimensions of life because he'd passed up Christ. One night, after a terrific internal struggle, he came forward and surrendered himself to Jesus. Later, he took me to dinner and effervesced with the life of Christ. The last I heard, he was spending his Sundays going from church to church telling people about how he had been newly born again.

Finally, anyone who hears Christ's call and responds can be born again! On the day of Pentecost, as 3,000 were about to surge forward to put their faith in Christ as Lord and become the initial nucleus of the Church, St. Peter implored: "Repent, and be baptized every one of you in the name of Jesus Christ for the remission of sins, and ye shall receive the gift of the Holy Ghost. For the promise is unto you, and to your children, and to all that are afar off, even as many as the Lord our God shall call" (Acts 2:38-39).

My wife, Kathleen, and three of our four boys were born in Ireland. I was asked to do a series of crusades there in Presbyterian churches when I was a research student. Accompanying me were the Gleaner Quartet. On the last night of the last crusade, Bobby Dunbar, the 2nd bass, asked Drew, the first tenor, to tell how he had been born again. Drew was a handsome 21-year-old with curly blue-black hair, but he had a chronic stutter. When he got up, his knees were knocking but somehow he got it said. He was brought up in a Christian home but despite being baptized and joining the church and having attended three times a week since childhood, he finished school and went to work for a stained glass window company without ever being born again. One afternoon, after having put Jesus Christ into a stained glass window, he was putting his tools away and preparing to punch out. The other workers had already gone.

Suddenly, it hit him, like the proverbial "ton of bricks," "I put Jesus Christ into this stained glass window, but I've never asked Him into my heart!"

At once he said, "Lord Jesus Christ, whom I put on the cross, by my sins, come down off the cross and into my heart and cleanse me from my sins by Thy blood. Come out of the stained glass window into which I put you today, and be my Lord and Saviour." He stood up. He was a new person—a real Christian. He had been born again, and he knew it.

That was the last night of those Presbyterian crusades. I came home to Canada for my father's funeral and three months later I was back in Ireland. I saw Bobby Dunbar on the sidewalk in Port Rush. I pulled the car over and said, "Bobby, how are you?"

"Fine."

"How's the quartet?"

"Didn't you hear about Drew?"

"No."

"Well, the night he gave his testimony was his last night of singing. That week the quartet met for practice. Drew's face was fading from its usual pink. He was also short of breath and he was missing on the high notes. They took him to the hospital and found he had leukemia. Three months later he was little more than skin and bones. The end was obviously at hand. The others in the quartet, Drew's parents, the doctor and the minister were standing around the bedside. Suddenly, the minister stepped forward, peeled back the flap on the oxygen tent and said, 'Drew, you're soon going to another world. Are you sure where you're going?' Opening his eyes and looking past the minister and straight into the eyes of his mother, he said, with a last flash of Irish humor, 'I wish I were as sure of my breakfast tomorrow morning.' Then waiting angel arms folded him home to the land beyond the sunset.''

He was heaven bound because he had been heaven born.

Chapter 6

What Keeps People from
Being Born Again?

Clearly, when all the pros and cons of being born again are weighed by any rational mind, one would think that all responsible people would be born again. But obviously, most of the population on planet earth are wittingly headed for hell. It seems such a tragedy. But it is true.

So we ask why? What keeps people from being born again?

In the first place the devil makes the prevention of rebirths his number one priority.

It used to be that very few sophisticated people would admit in broad daylight that they believed in the existence of a real, live, personal devil. Today, that's all changed. A *Redbook* survey of 65,000 Americans in 1977 reveals that 78% of those polled believed in the personality of Satan. In another North American polling, it was revealed that 4 1/2 times as many people believe in a personal devil as voted for President Carter in the 1976 election. Eleven percent more believe in his reality now than 15 years ago.

Earlier in the decade, Arthur Lyons wrote *The Second Coming: Satanism in America,* and for doing so, perambulated from Johnny Carson to Mike Douglas like a mailman going house to house. The devil rates cover stories and feature articles in *Newsweek, Time* and *The New York Times.* He has climbed visibly and vocally far enough out of perdition to beget churches of Satan around the world and to be a more legitimate theme of study and prayer in many school systems than God Almighty. Recently the *Toronto Star* had a feature article on the astonishing number of "Lawyers, doctors, actors, designers and businessmen who are joining what used to be the underground culture studying the fascinating world" of Satanism. In Europe, Asia and Africa, from Galway to Vladivostok and from Lapland to Madras, Satanism is saturating whole communities in a manner which hasn't occurred since the Dark Ages. Latin America is a hotbed of societies dominated by the occult. As Pope Paul puts it, "The world today is being terrorized by a Satan who is a terrible reality, overpowering communities and entire societies around the world." The Pope points to Satan as the prince of this world, the number one enemy, with an army of occupation composed of an awestriking plurality of demon hosts.

St. Paul assured us that "in the latter times" there'd be a dramatic escalation in those who'd be "giving heed unto seducing spirits and doctrines of devils" (1 Tim. 4:1). Certainly Satan is a hot theme in the media. He captivates the screen not only with the record-breaking film "The Exorcist," which grossed 50 million dollars, but "Exorcism's Daughter," "The Demons," "The Devil in Mrs. Jones," "Dracula, Satan's Rib," "Satan Is Coming," "The Legions of Lucifer," "The Devil's Wedding Night," and "The Devil's Doorway."

Currently, *The Los Angeles Times,* probably closer than any other newspaper to Hollywood films, states that films are, in a sense, a monitor of modern man's mind moods. Notes *The Times:* "It seems that Satan has become the patron saint of many movie producers who have discovered that Armageddon has a more successful box office climate than *Shangri-la."* "To the Devil, a Daughter," says *The Times,* "is only the latest offering in the burgeoning field of film demonology."

Other current films featuring the devil are "The Devil's Playground," featuring mymphettes fulfilling all of Satan's erotic desires; "Beyond the Door"; where, we're assured, "demoniac possession lives, and grows"; and "Psychic Killer," which introduces the viewer to the "Master of Evil" who "drives 'em mad, then he kills, kills and kills." Add to this, "Race with the Devil," "The Devil's Rain," "God Told Me To"—a blasphemous depiction of the Antichrist, who allegedly was born on December 25, 1951, and "Helter Skelter," a satanic review of "The Manson Massacres."

Surely such offerings confirm what Jesus said of religious people, who had never been born again: "Ye are of your father the devil, and the lusts of your father ye will do. He was a murderer from the beginning, and abode not in the truth, because there is no truth in him. When he speaketh a lie, he speaketh of his own: for he is a liar, and the father of it" (John 8:44).

But there is immediate, sure and eternal victory over Satan and all his evil hosts through total surrender to Jesus Christ. In 1 John 4:4, where the battle for the soul between Satan and our Saviour is clearly set forth, we read: "Greater is he [Jesus] that is in you than he [Satan] that is in the world." St. Peter assured us that while our "adversary the devil, as a roaring lion, walketh about, seeking whom he may devour," in Christ we confront him squarely and "resist steadfast in the faith" (1 Pet. 5:8-9).

The distinguished British surgeon psychiatrist Dr. Kenneth McAll recently toured Canada. He believes millions of people today are demon possessed, and billions in the devil's corral. He says that through invoking the power of Christ, he's seen, in hundreds of instances, in Asia, in Britain and here in North America, the powers of Satan totally dispelled.

I was addressing a convention of medical doctors in Missouri, and Dr. B. L. Boatright told me of a 25-year-old who had come home from the army. He had gone on hard drugs and opened himself up to demonization. Breaking off with his wife and two children, when he arrived home, he was desolate. So he slashed his wrists. Sewing them up, Dr. Boatright told him how to open his life to Christ. Receiving Jesus, he was born again and given grace to get himself and his family together again and to go with Christ and His church.

I was in a recent crusade in a hockey arena in the Midwest. Into the Saturday evening crusade meeting came the beautiful blond daughter of a clergyman. Her hair was down to her waist. She was religiously turned off, deeply into Satan worship, tripping out on drugs and sexually sleeping around. She did *not* come forward to confess Christ. Instead, she went to the Country Kitchen for coffee. But Jesus "followed her," and she returned to the arena where a kindly counsellor led her to Christ.

A second thing that keeps people from being born again is sin.

Since the Garden of Eden, sin has always been the

separator between God and man. God simply will not compromise His holiness by permitting a person who will not repent of sin to experience the new birth. And as long as a man won't turn from his sin to trust Christ, there is no way God Almighty will save him. Our whole pleasure mad generation is oriented toward sin—both crime and personal sins. For instance, it is a chief theme on TV. Harold Hastings writes in the *Los Angeles Times*: "My two teen-aged sons have learned a great deal from television. Every night they are taught how to steal, to rape, to outwit police, to hold up banks, to shoot dope, to escape from speeding police cars and to commit murder." Like the days of Noah, or the society of Sodom and Gomorrah, the whole mind set of our generation is toward sin.

However, once a person turns to Christ to forgive him of his sin, there is no sin so big which Christ won't or can't forgive. We received a letter from a lady which reads: "For the last eleven years my husband and I have been so lost. Living in constant sin, we were blaming the other for our sins. My husband was being possessed by alcohol and I was an adulteress, but praise God, these devils no longer live in our hearts, bodies or souls." Then they together watched one of our telecasts and the lady continues that as a result "we found Jesus. We asked for forgiveness of our sins; we confessed with our mouths the Lord Jesus, and asked for salvation. Jesus came into our hearts and gave us eternal peace. This is the greatest gift we have ever known. By God's grace we are saved. We are reborn."

A third thing that keeps people from being born again is a rejection of the love of God.

God loved us by Christ's coming to the cross. But such a provision of love is only a completed circuit when the recipient responds.

I was driving along in my car the other day and heard a disc jockey say that the Spanish have six words for saying "I love you!" and that we in English have only one word. The Greeks had four words for love: *eros*—sensual love; *storgay*—family love; *Philia*—brotherly love; and *Agape*—God's pure and perfect love. It was almost a forgotten word in the Greek. Then God, who is love, sent His Son. And evangelists wanting to write about it found this incomparable word *Agape* and wrote gospels and epistles about Jesus Christ. In the New Testament, *Agape* love is to be found 250 times.

And man today is nearly love starved. A headline reads: "Doctors need to be loved too!" Psychiatrist Howard Kern says that what doctors need more than money, or success, or recognition is to be loved! People spend a lifetime looking for love. The celebrated Rona Jaffe was asked why she had never married. Her rather sad answer was: "I didn't love any of the men who asked me to marry them; and the ones I loved never asked!" Insofar as your spiritual wedding to Christ is concerned, He both loves you *and* asks you.

Sigmund Freud observed: "Love is the first requirement for mental health." Reflected Victor Hugo: "The supreme happiness of life is the conviction that we are loved." Bertrand Russell wrote that the one pursuit of his life was for love. He never found it. John Lennon, the Beatle, said that his obsessive quest for fame was a quest for the love that had been denied him as a child in Liverpool. His father never appeared till he was 20. With his mother out at work, he was kicked around the neighborhood like a half flattened soccer ball. So the Beatles rode to fame singing such songs as: "All You Need Is Love" and "I Can't Live in a World Without Love." In an article recently on

Carole Burnett, Lucille Ball and herself, Joan Rivers remarked: "There's no comedian, man or woman, who didn't start out feeling lonely or unloved."

So our generation pursues love. Jaqueline Susanne writes *The Love Machine*. But love isn't a machine. Vincent Toro and Louise Heath win a trip to Canada from Florida for kissing in public for a consecutive 92 hours, 32 minutes and 3 seconds. But love isn't a kissing marathon. I heard a song on the CBC recently which went: "God Loves You When You Smile!" Yes —but sometimes His love only gets to us when we cry. "Whom the Lord loveth he chasteneth, and scourgeth every son whom he receiveth," wrote the writer to the Hebrews (12:6). John Locke, the English philosopher more responsible for the political principles behind the American Republic than any other, once mused: "If you bore deeply enough into the earth, you'll strike water. And if you bore deeply enough into the human heart, you'll strike tears."

I was in a crusade in Ashland, Oregon, on the West Coast. From California, to get her away from her nest of gold, Ann had been brought by friends with tender loving care to our crusade. She had been living in a modern meadow of lush greenbacks. But dollar bills couldn't fulfill her spiritual needs. At the age of 23, a stunning, beautiful blond, she had given birth to the only baby her doctor told her she could ever have. But the baby died, and she felt she had no reason to live, so she had tried to end it all with an overdose. Discovered, still alive, Ann had been rushed to the hospital and a quick tracheotomy performed. Three weeks later she was brought to our crusade. I presented Christ as the source of love and she was born again.

Finally, what keeps people from being born again is neglect.

Many a person inside as well as outside the church

neglects the Word of Christ in the Gospel.

Joe Conlee was brought up on an Iowa farm. To please his parents he became a Methodist clergyman. But he had neglected the one thing he needed most. He had never been born again.

Times were hard on the prairie, so he went to California.

Though he was a spell-binding orator pastoring huge congregations, he finally had to announce: "My friends, I am about to make a confession. I can no longer believe the Bible. This is the last time I will ever preach." Though he wrote for and later edited several famous newspapers, he gave it all up to sink down into skidrow and booze. A Christian doctor who once had been in his congregation discovered him and gave him a ticket to the Yukon, where, it was hoped, he might change. A prospector gave him a job as lookout guard in the Lonely Log Cabin, 40 miles from Dawson City. His wages were to be groceries, a pile of logs for his pot-belly stove, and a huge wooden barrel of his favorite whiskey.

It was edging into winter and the whiskey barrel was a quarter empty when Jimmy Miller, a lapsed Roman Catholic, knocked on the door. Within two weeks, Wally Flett, a spiritualist medium from San Francisco, had checked into the Lonely Cabin also and the three of them exchanged obscenities, munched a little food, stoked up the fire, and stayed continuously stoned.

But the party went awry one night when Jimmy Miller woke up screaming: "Get me a doctor! Get me a doctor! You can't just let me lie here and die!" His delirium tremens had shot him into a near fatal fever. But it was 40° below. A terrible blizzard was howling outside and hungry wolves were looking for victims. Then Joe remembered. He had a little medicine chest which his wife had packed for him. Rolling the contents out on the filthy, dishevelled floor, out tumbled a Bible with a note: "Daddy, Mommy put in a little medicine chest that she thought you might need if you should get hurt there. We will pray for you. And Daddy, inside the medicine chest I have put my little Book. I wouldn't give it to anybody else in the world but you. You read it." Signed, Flory.

Joe lumbered over to the pot-belly stove to throw in the Bible when Wally Flett cut him off: "What you got, Conlee?"

"It's a Bible, curse it!"

"Don't throw it in, man! Don't you know we haven't got a thing to read in this God-forsaken country? Your only magazine I have read twenty times."

So Wally Flett, the spiritualist, grabbed little Flory's Bible and began to read it aloud to Jimmy Miller, while Joe gave him the medicines. Joe cursed the reading, but Jimmy said he had to have it to get well. Within a month the three were reading in turns. The cursings lessened and the whiskey level went down more slowly.

Christmas came and went. Finally, on Valentine's Day, the unlikely troika reached John 14. That February 14 Wally read: "Let not your heart be troubled: ye believe in God, believe also in me. In my Father's house are many mansions: if it were not so, I would have told you." By the time he got to verse 6, Joe was on his knees, behind the pot-belly stove, trying to hide his tears. Jimmy was kneeling beside the creaky horse-blanketed bed. And as Wally read that 6th verse, "I am the way, the truth, and the life," Jesus himself drew near. Three old drunken cronies were visited by the presence—the real presence—of the Man with the seamless robe and the nail-pierced hands. And when a new day dawned, Joe, Jimmy, and Wally were new creations in Christ Jesus. Their long neglect had ended. And when spring arrived they came south, telling the world that they had been born again in Christ.

Chapter 7

When Can You be Born Again?

One of the most exciting prospects for a married couple is the birth of a baby. When will it be born? They confer with their doctor and he sets a likely date, give or take a few days. And with eagerness they look forward to the hour of the newborn's arrival.

When can a person be born again spiritually? The ideal time is when the Gospel is preached.

Christmas 1965, I drove Kathleen and our four boys home to celebrate on the farm at Pangman, Saskatchewan, where my brother Lewis lives and where I was born. And during those Christmas holidays we held a Billy Graham Crusade in Eston where I have so many lifelong friends. It was the closing weekend, and on Saturday Kathleen went to get her hair done and she took our 6-year-old Randy, who didn't like the altered style and announced: "My stupid old mother. I'm not going to sit with her tonight!" The beautician asked him where it was that he wouldn't be sitting with his mother, and got an invitation to come to the crusade. Not only did the lady come, she listened to the Word of Christ being preached and came forward to be born again there in the high school gymnasium. The next night she was back with her husband, and he too came forward to be born again in Christ. Their hearts five months earlier had been tenderized by the death of their little child.

Of course, there are those who are born again, having been led directly to Christ by the personal witness of someone who takes a spiritual interest in them. In John 1:40-42 we read that "Andrew, Simon Peter's brother . . . first findeth his own brother Simon, and saith unto him, We have found the Messias, which is, being interpreted, the Christ. And he brought him to Jesus."

A few years ago in Connecticut a Roman Catholic priest led Betty Hutton, the ex-film star, into an experience of being born again. Her testimony spread as far around the world as her films had flung her face and figure. It was a simple straightforward "I have found the Christ"—the same as Andrew's.

I was recently preaching in a crusade, and Professor George Smock came to give his testimony. His father was a professor of English, and George followed in his academic footprints, but was looking for other spiritual footsteps in which to walk. He abandoned academe to become a hippy in Haight Ashbury. Still disillusioned, he went to Africa in quest of a messiah. He stood naked at night on African beaches, trying to rendezvous with the moon. There was no communication. Then one day a little, nearly illiterate black boy told George in broken English the story of Jesus Christ, His atonement on the cross, and how to be saved. George knelt down on African sand and gave himself to Jesus. Today, he preaches Christ as well as teaching English.

Often people are born again through a combination of personal witness and preaching. Sometimes the witnessing comes first, then the preaching. At other times, the preaching precedes the witnessing. I love

to hear George Beverly Shea tell about his commitment to Christ in his father's church in Ottawa.
It was the last night with Evangelist Fred Suffield.
Bev was 18, and sat in the very back corner seat of
the church. As the invitation was extended to come
to Christ, Mr. Shea, Sr., slipped down the aisle, put
his hand on Bev's shoulder and said: "Son, do you
think tonight might be the night?" It was. George
Beverly Shea began that night with Jesus Christ, and
has presented Him face to face to more people than
any other Canadian ever has.

When can you be born again? When you are led
into such an experience by reading the Scriptures or
reading a book which includes a great number of
Scriptures. Jesus said plainly that "it is the Spirit that
quickeneth [brings life]; the flesh profiteth nothing:
the words that I speak unto you, they are Spirit, and
they are life" (John 6:63). Napoleon once confessed,
to his own chagrin, that when we confront the Word
of God, we are not encountering a dead book but a
living Creation.

Frank Orr, the sports columnist, wrote the widely
quoted account of how Paul Henderson was born
again, for sports fans throughout the world to read.
He described Paul as one of the half dozen best-
known Canadians in the world by virtue of his having
scored by far the most thrilling three goals in the history of hockey. The occasion was when Team Canada
beat Team Russia in that hockey Everest in 1972.
However, Paul's journey to the pinnacle of fame and
adulation bottomed out to a nadir of depression, when
three years later his leg was smashed up and, in
Paul's own words, "For almost eight weeks in that
cast, I hardly went out of the house. I had time to
read and think for the first time—and the opportunity
to reassess my life. I asked myself: Where am I?

I'd always been a fairly religious person, but in a pretty casual sort of a way. In trying to find the answers, I realized that I'd have to get back to the only truly solid values. That's when I committed my life to Christ." Paul's testimony has since been heralded far and wide: a confirmation of how the Word of God (along with helpful literature) is a means of bringing spiritual rebirth.

When can you be born again? When you hear the call of Christ.

It is a pathetic thing when someone is lost in the dark and hears no call or spiritually sees no light. Rock guitarist Eric Clapton of Black Summer Rain fame laments: "I just can't find the sun in my life." What Eric needs is the Son of God to call to him, and for him to respond.

I was in a crusade in a football stadium in Tennessee a few years ago. On to the track in front of the stands was rolled a wheelchair with a 71-year-old man who was blind, deaf and dumb. His sister tapped out in morse code on the back of his hand my sermon, and at the end I asked those who wished to respond to Christ's call to repeat after me. He asked to be pushed forward with the other inquirers and tapped out onto his sister's hand the prayer of commitment to Christ. He intimated that he had been born again.

When can you be born again? When the Holy Spirit is speaking to you, convincing you of your sin and calling you to Christ. Professor Tholuck, the German, was asked what God's second greatest gift to man was, and he replied, "The Holy Spirit who convicts us of our sins so that we will come to God's greatest gift, His only begotten Son." When Jesus was announcing to His disciples the coming of the Holy Spirit, He declared that "when he is come, he will reprove the world of sin, and of righteousness, and of judgment:

of sin, because they believe not on me; of righteousness, because I go to my Father, and ye see me no more; of judgment, because the prince of this world is judged" (John 16:9-11). The conviction of the Holy Spirit is the most powerful and explicit force in the human spirit that I know anything about. And, it is increased by the prayers of God's people.

In the Midwest I was preaching on the text: "Jesus called unto Him His disciples." Eighteen-year-old Terri Parks came forward to be born again that particular night. Three nights later, with tears of rejoicing and gratitude, she came up to me after the service and told me that on the night she made her response to Christ, her 83-year-old grandmother was in the meeting. She had prayed for her all her life and often told her she should become a Christian. She had been there to see her granddaughter's response and hear her testimony. At dawn the next morning, she died and went to heaven, content that the Spirit had done His work.

Sometimes this conviction of the Holy Spirit can be extraordinarily personal. Recently I received a letter from a nurse named Elizabeth. She was sitting with her friend Mary, and I was preaching the Gospel and inviting people to make their decisions for Christ. She wrote: "You said, 'God actually calls people very often by their name,' and then you said . . . 'Elizabeth, Mary.' " She said she thought if she didn't respond there and then, she might go out and get killed. Well, both she and Mary said "yes" to Jesus, and they've since been living born-again lives. Then there was the college student, Phil Realing, who came forward in a meeting in Wyoming. Every night for a week he attended, telling me at the end why he had come to Christ: "I felt the Lord nudging me!" He was obviously feeling the conviction of the Holy Spirit strongly.

Finally: *when* can you be born again? *Now* is God's time. One of the most balanced verses in all of the Bible in this regard is 2 Corinthians 6:2. "Behold, now is the accepted time; behold, now is the day of salvation." Sir Walter Scott declared: "The three most important letters in the English language are N-O-W!"

The crucial thing we must be aware of is that we never know how brief our remaining time cn earth may be.

Recently I was out speaking in Westway United Church in Toronto with my friend Reverend Vic Wood. Eric Montgomery came up to me afterwards and recalled that when we had the crusade in the Islington Hockey arena there in 1967, his 22-year-old daughter, who has since gone to be with Christ, had a girlfriend whose mother had immigrated from England. Her name was Mrs. Alf Daniels. She was brought to the crusade and came forward to give her life to Jesus Christ. Though she was only in her 40s, she had cancer, and within a few short weeks she emigrated again—this time to heaven.

In the mid-seventies, I was conducting a crusade in a mountain city in Washington State. One Sunday night, Billy Joe McGlassen, 12 years old, strode out of his seat to the front and received and confessed Jesus Christ as his Lord and Saviour. Two months later I found out that Billy Joe, the day before, had been out with his school class on a science trip. It was noon, up on the Saddle Rock Cliff. One of Billy Joe's friends was about to eat his bag lunch when the bag slipped out of his hand and toward the edge of the cliff. Billy Joe selflessly made a lunge for his friend's lunch. In doing so, he fell over the edge to his death, but up into everlasting life, with Christ. I sat down and wrote a letter of comfort to Billy Joe's parents. I shall always treasure his mother's letter of response. She grieved that he had been taken early, but rejoiced in the realization he had been born again.

Chapter 8

How Can You Know
That You've Been Born Again?

It is imperative that a believer in Christ have assurance that he or she has been born again. Assurance of salvation is not a luxury that a Christian aspires to. It is a necessity for spiritual health. Insecurity, any psychologist knows, is one of the most unwholesome hazards that can jeopardize any human relationship within society. How much more important it is that we have spiritual assurance that we have been born again. One of the most perilous parent/child crises that can arise is for the child to develop doubt about his actual relationship to his parents. One of the most perilous Christ/believer crises that can arise is for doubt to creep in as to whether or not there is a sure relationship. "The effect of righteousness," avowed Isaiah (32:17), is "quietness and assurance forever." "Our gospel came not unto you in word only," asserted St. Paul to the Thessalonians, "but in power, and in the Holy Ghost, and in much assurance" (1 Thess. 1:5).

The first principle of assurance is the pledge of Christ from the cross. When Jesus was on that cross He cried: "Father, forgive them; for they know not what they do" (Luke 23:34), and a little later: "It is finished" (John 19:30)—one word in the Greek, meaning, "paid for." Jesus completed the transaction of atoning for our sins on the cross—totally!

Assurance of salvation rests on the fact of Christ being risen from the dead. "Our Lord Jesus Christ," wrote St. Peter, "hath begotten us again unto a lively hope by the resurrection of Jesus Christ from the dead" (1 Pet. 1:3).

The late Karl Barth of Switzerland, foremost name theologian of this century, stated before his death that "if you deny the physical resurrection of Jesus Christ, you have no Christianity left." When in the last century the same question arose, and the opinion of Englishman, Thomas Arnold, that great Rugby scholar, was asked, he replied, "The resurrection of Jesus Christ from the dead is the best proven fact in history." When I was working on my Doctor of Philosophy degree at Oxford, I was in Mansfield College, whose founder was the venerated Dr. R. W. Dale. The great moment in his life, the one in which he always, thereafter, claimed he was born again, came when he was about to speak one Easter Sunday in Birmingham. As he was about to ascend into his pulpit, suddenly the fact "Jesus is alive!" seized him, and he was never the same again. His church filled. His fame spread throughout the world, and the whole future of his generation, because of the influence he exerted, changed direction for the better.

There is no way to know Christ without the realization that He rose from the dead and is currently and forever alive. You see, you can be a Confucionist without ever having known Confucius. You can be Moslem without ever having known Mohammed, and you can be a Buddhist without ever having known

Buddha. But you cannot be a Christian without knowing Christ.

Some months ago I was holding a crusade in the upper Midwest. The day I arrived in that city, I read of the tragic death in an automobile accident of 19-year-old Dale Kmett. His mother, Ruth, obviously was brokenhearted. But the tragedy also opened her heart, and being brought to the crusade, she came forward to receive the risen, living Christ into her forlorn heart.

Assurance that you've been born again rests on the Word of God. In fact, that is why the Bible was written. It's God's love letter to you to tell you how you can know that you're His. I John 5:13 states, "These things have I written unto you that believe on the name of the Son of God; that ye may know that ye have eternal life."

To me, it is a remarkable thing that so many in this very insecure moment in history are turning again to the Scriptures. Year after year, the Bible is the world's best seller. Barbara Bennett puts it: "God's Word is like a pencil sharpener. It gives my life a point." It seems that in the late seventies, the press, the theater and the world of scholarship have all been abuzz with the number of confirmations of the dependability of the Scriptures which have been surfacing. One headline states: "By 1996 . . . the Bible will be proved true." Another reads: "500 Top Scientists Believe That the Bible Story of Creation Is True." Another: "Discovery in Syria Backs Up the Bible." The latter headline refers to the archaeological find of 15,000 clay tablets, 4,000 years old, which seem to be the full of heretofore nonexistent extrabiblical proofs that Old Testament history is indeed accurate. Names like Abraham, Esau, Israel, Saul and Jerusalem are there in their original form.

Then there has been the feature film: "In Search of Noah's Ark," which has been presented in theaters, coast to coast, a very convincing case for the extant existence of a mammoth Ark, exactly as the Bible described in Genesis 6. George Gallup in his poll of the people was astonished at the very high percentage, both of Protestants and Catholics, who believe that the Bible is the inspired, trustworthy and authoritative Word of God.

I was preaching in the ACC arena of Notre Dame University in Indiana in 1975. A school teacher, Maude Klingaman, was so confused about her spiritual state that her teaching had deteriorated drastically. She wrote to me later about how, one night, she got up courage, came to the front and was born again in Christ. She further wrote: "The Lord you apoke about is real salvation. The guilt, loneliness and emptiness are gone. The promises of God are real. The Scriptures have come alive for me. . . . The Holy Spirit worked a miracle in my life." And Maude Klingaman's classes became a living experience, rather than just a job.

John Wesley, two centuries ago, attached maximal importance to the assurance of salvation being communicated through the witness of the Holy Spirit. In Romans 8:16 we read, "The Spirit himself beareth witness with our spirit, that we are the children of God."

In response to our television program, "Agape," a young lady wrote to tell us of her being born again when she prayed the prayer of commitment to Christ at the end. A part of Lori's letter reads: "I always thought highly of myself because I get good marks in school. Last week was the first time I really was interested and believed in God and Jesus. When I prayed with you, I suddenly had a bubbly feeling inside. It felt as if someone was lightening me up. Now I BELIEVE." And she capitalized "BE-LIEVE." That's exactly what Jesus promised: "He who believes in me, out of his heart shall flow rivers of living water" (Lori calls it bubbles). "This he said about the Spirit," wrote St. John, who comes to us when we believe (John 7:37-39).

A further evidence that we've been born again is a love for Christians. "By this shall all men know that ye are my disciples, if ye have love one to another" (John 13:35), said Jesus to His followers.

Perhaps the most conspicuous example of how Christ turns hate for Christians into love can be seen in the experience of Eldridge Cleaver, co-founder of the Black Panthers, and from the age of 19 to 41, a dedicated Marxist. His disdain for his country, his fellow citizenry, and for God became so acid that he decided to travel the communist world and seek support for an eventual revolutionary overthrow of the United States. But he ended up thoroughly disillusioned. One night, in the south of France, a remarkable thing happened. He relates it in his own words.

"I was looking up at the moon and I saw the man in the moon . . . and it was my face. . . . Then I saw that the face was not mine, but some of my old heroes. There was Fidel Castro; then there was Mao Tse Tung. While I watched, the face turned to Jesus Christ and I was very much surprised. . . . I don't know when I had last cried, but I began to cry and I didn't stop. I was still crying and I got on my knees and said the Lord's Prayer. I remembered that, and then I said the 23rd Psalm because my mother taught me that, too. It was like I could not stop crying unless I said the prayer and the Psalm and surrendered something. All I had to do was surrender and go to jail." At that point he returned to the United States. In prison, Eldridge put his hand on the New Testament and said: "Jesus, this is Eldridge Cleaver." And Jesus flashed back: "Eldridge, this is Jesus." At the 1977 Presidential Prayer Breakfast in Washington, Eldridge Cleaver and Charles Colson both shared the testimony of having been born again in Christ. From the President of the United States, to the humblest viewer of the television news, it was evident that here were men who once hated each other and everything the other represented—now one in Christ Jesus and loving each other in a manner that only their being born again could explain.

Finally, you know you're born again by the fruit of the Spirit in your life. John the Baptist exhorted responding believers to "bring forth therefore fruits meet for repentance" (Matt. 3:8).

Spiritual fruit-bearing takes various forms. It may take someone to the ends of the earth to evangelize. Back in August, 1974, I was riding a crowded train in Lausanne, Switzerland, when the World Congress on Evangelism was being held there. Elizabeth Egli sat down beside me. She told me how her family moved from the German to the French sector of Switzerland when she was 14. Not only could she not speak the language, she had T.B. She was crying herself to sleep one night when Jesus, the Light of the World, came to claim her. She said, "Yes." Five or six years later, while in nurses training in the South of England, Jesus came to her again and put His finger on Niger, one of the tragic famine countries on the south side of the Sahara. Would she go? She said, "Yes. If I'm asked." Shortly after, she was asked by a mission board director to go—of all places on the globe—to Niger. Now she was like a humming-bird on a birch branch, binding up the wounds of the starving; feeding, clothing and housing the pathetic poor of Niger, and telling them about the Light of the World, Jesus.

Then there are those whose fruit-bearing is in a supportive ministry. In May, 1971, a millionaire fruit farmer by the name of Howard Howe, aged 62, came forward in a crusade I was conducting in Florida. Thereafter, his life was full of fruit-bearing for Christ. Five years later, a mutual friend was having breakfast with me and told of how Howard was a completely transformed man, giving hugely of his resources to evangelize the world. Then one day, he went into one of his orchards on a tractor to pull a stump. The tractor overturned. When they found Howard, he was crushed to death under his tractor. But he was safe in the arms of Jesus, because he had been born again.

Chapter 9

What Effect Does Being Born Again Have on the Individual?

It is often asked, "What effect for good does being born again have on the individual?"

In the first place, there is a deep love for Christ in the heart of everyone who has genuinely been born again. St. John wrote that "we love him, because he first loved us" (1 John 4:19).

There's a song topping the pops, "You're the First, the Last, My Everything." To the believer, Jesus Christ is "the First, the Last, My Everything."

When we lived in Oxford, I drove down to Devonshire in the South of England. A boy, dying from leukemia, received Jesus as his Saviour and Lord. As he was lying there, his sister was in attendance and suddenly he came up on his frail elbows and exclaimed: "Bring!" His sister ran and got his father. The lad shook his head. But soon he rose up again and gasped: "Bring!" This time she rushed in with a glass of water. Again he shook his head. But then he rose up a final time before going silent, as angel arms folded him home to the land above the stars. But this time he exclaimed: "Bring forth the royal diadem and crown Him—Lord of all!" Even in dying, this lad had one thing uppermost in his mind—his love for Christ.

I received a letter recently from a lady who had contemplated suicide. She lamented, "I can't go on." But she saw our "Agape" program on television. She wrote, "Today I received Jesus into my heart. I have run the gamut of the psychiatrists for almost twenty years. Today I have committed my life to Christ. I must have Him as my Lord. I do love Him, and *now*, whatever He says, goes." Signed, Diane.

What Diane had experienced when she was born again was a love for Christ.

A few hours prior to this writing, my son and I were driving through Detroit and saw a truck with its I.D. "New Life Feed" painted onto its big box. The second evidence that a person has been born again is a hunger for the Word of God: for "New Life Feed," if you will! St. Peter put it: "As new-born babes, desire the sincere milk of the word, that ye may grow thereby" (1 Pet. 2:2).

As Pat Boone puts it: "The Bible is as current and immediate as today's newspaper—and a lot more accurate. It should be: it was programmed," says Pat, "by the same heavenly computer that hung the stars."

Back in the sixties, I was preaching in a stadium in Idaho. A frail little lady with several small children who lived in one squalid room with a drunken husband came forward one night to be born again. A minister went and called on her a few days later and found her reading the Bible when he entered, and her face lit up as she said, "You know, when I opened my life to Christ, it was like switching on the light in our home and when the light goes on, the darkness goes out."

Another effect of being born again, in the life of

the believer, is a thirst to be filled with the Holy Spirit. In John 4, Jesus had introduced the harlot of Samaria to the water of eternal life. In John 7:37-39 we read that He issued another invitation: "Jesus stood and cried, saying, If any man thirst, let him come unto me, and drink. He that believeth on me, as the scripture hath said, out of his [innermost being] shall flow rivers of living water.... This spake he of the Spirit, which they that believe on him should receive." Beginning on the Day of Pentecost, the day the Church was born, believers began to receive the very special gift of the Holy Spirit whom Jesus said (in this unique way) "was not yet given" (John 7:39), for He was still on earth incarnate. But from Acts 2, onward, whenever Christ was preached and people believed on the Lord Jesus Christ and were saved, thereafter they would have a thirst to be filled with the Holy Spirit.

One of the remarkable conversions of the mid-seventies was that of the world's most celebrated cook, Graham Kerr, known through the English-speaking world as "The Galloping Gourmet." For twenty years, Graham has been turning talk shows and television studios into cooking kitchens and dramatically sharpening human appetites. One of the world's most gifted communicators, he has charmed millions. While living near Washington, he and his wife Teena had a tragic accident. For three years they wrestled adversity. Then Teena was miraculously born again. Graham had tried desperately to resist conversion, preferring to rely on materialistic success and his ego mania, as he puts it. But it was like "putting a Band-Aid on a volcano." Then on March 13, 1975, in his Ottawa motel room, after 14 hours on the television set, he opened a Bible, and within a few moments, became a Christian. In his own words: "I began praying and suddenly blurted out: 'Jesus, I love you.' There are no words for what I then experienced. It was as if the whole ceiling was unzipped and I was being reached down to and held. There was a warm glowing feeling all over and all my weariness slipped away. I began praising God, and I've been doing it ever since." Now, to millions on television, to thousands in auditoriums, and to individuals, Graham and Teena Kerr are telling about Jesus and how their inner thirst has been satisfied by the power of the Holy Spirit.

Another effect of being born again is an inner desire for holiness.

When one becomes a born-again Christian, he turns from his sin.

I received a letter from a long-term convict, converted to Christ through watching "Agape." He wrote that, having "accepted Christ as my Saviour, He was responsible for pulling me away from an addiction to heroin, speed and cocaine. I was very badly hooked when Christ came into my life and filled me with His Spirit. At that time I weighed 110 pounds and not even my parents could recognize me. It's been nine months now since Christ saved me and I now weigh 160 pounds and I've got a reason to live! Christ showed me a better life and I've got a reason to live."

Another effect of being a born-again Christian is an irrepressible urge to tell others about Christ.

"Being a witness for Christ," says Billy Graham, "is neither optional nor mandatory; rather, it is inevitable." But when one witnesses for Christ, he must learn that he, like a turtle, must begin by sticking out his neck and getting his mouth open. So a witness for Christ will pray till the tears come, work till the sweat comes, and give till it hurts. The debt he owes God, he'll pay to needy people around him.

I think that the closest I've ever been to heaven and, ironically enough, to hell, was during a visit in the Philippines to what is reputedly the world's largest (and surely one of the most wretched) prisons. Olga Robertson was an Arab woman who, during World War II, had been disenfranchised by her wealthy upper-class parents when she married an American by the name of Robertson at Clark Air Force Base. Olga was pregnant with twins when Robertson went home to the United States. She never saw him again. Feeling completely forsaken, she headed for the Pacific to drown herself and her babies. En route she heard music and went into a mission and gave her life to Jesus. While praying, she felt a call to take Christ into that terrible prison. Now, thirty years later, she is its beloved chaplain. After our meeting, she took me to the electric chair room and to death row. She told me of a young man called Billy who had recently been executed for murdering two people. Prior to his execution she had led him to Christ during a meeting on death row. Before he died, he donated both his eyes to an eye bank, was shaved, hooded, and with the electrodes tight into his head sang, "Yea, though I walk through the valley of the shadow of death, I will fear no evil: for thou art with me" (Ps. 23:4). For him, death was just a shadow. Then he exulted: "Dear Jesus, I thank you that I am in your care and that you have prepared a place for me in heaven and I am going to see you face-to—" He never finished the sentence. He was in heaven. The death switch had been thrown.

From the electric chair room, Olga took me to death row itself. Every man there was condemned to die: some very soon. President Marcos was catching up on a backlog of executions. It seemed like a human zoo. There was crying and groaning. There was bitterness and hate. The ceiling was low. The heat was about a 100—and so was the humidity! The inmates slept and ate on the floor. The stench of the mingled vomit, urine, perspiration, and human excrement was indescribable. "This," I thought, "is the closest I've ever been to hell." Olga called for the death row "Jesus Trio" to step forward. Until Billy's death it had been a quartet. She told me afterwards that among them they had murdered perhaps a hundred people. Out of that squalid, terrified company stepped Romeo, Gaugenzio and Boyzeo. One had a beaten-up guitar. They opened their dog-eared songbook and sang in such angelic harmony, it was as if they were already in heaven. And they transported me from what felt like upstairs from hell to the ground floor of heaven.

Come ye sinners, poor and needy
Jesus' blood can make you free
For He saved the worst among us
When He saved a wretch like me.
Oh, I know, I surely know
That Jesus' blood can make the vilest sinner clean
Oh, I know, I surely know
That Jesus' blood can make the vilest sinner clean.

Chapter 10

What Effect Does Being Born Again Register in Society?

One of the chief controversies in the organized Church is whether society is changed for the better, more through the individuals of which it consists, or whether the system itself needs redemption and regeneration. Does transformation of society begin at the top and filter downward, or does it begin at the bottom and penetrate upward?

Jesus had a lot to say about believers in society. He bequeathed a very solemn responsibility to His followers. They were to be like light penetrating darkness. Like salt penetrating the whole body of society. Like a key penetrating the lock of a secular community; a leaven that would leaven the whole lump. Society today is flat. It needs to rise. The Church of Jesus Christ is always to be a life giver in an otherwise dying environment.

The born-again believer is a transformed person, not only from God's perspective, but also from that of an ever-observant society.

Paul Harvey, the noted newscaster, who professed to be born again about twenty years ago, was asked if Jesus ever really walked in the slums. "Yes," he replied, with even more than his usual candid deliberation; "more than any other reformer in history. The poor heard Him gladly, and He ate, and was found with sinners. But Jesus Christ didn't make the mistake of many modern reformist politicians. He never took the people out of the slums until He took the slums out of the people. This He, and He alone, could do, because He came as God the Son to be the Saviour of the world."

In Hyde Park, London, where anybody can say anything about anyone with virtually no restrictions, a born-again Christian was on one soapbox and next to him on another was a Communist. As both vied for the attention of the crowd, the Marxist spotted a disheveled tramp who looked like a ragbag broken open. Pointing at him, he pledged pompously: "Communism could put a new suit of clothes on that man!" The Christian replied, "Yes, Communism—or Capitalism—could put a new suit of clothes on that man. But Jesus Christ can put a new man in that suit of clothes!"

He's offering to make new people out of us. Mrs. Ghandi tried nobly to effect her dream but failed. "Indian society must be transformed." That's a prerogative which belongs uniquely to Jesus Christ. He has a monopoly on transformation. Canadians may aspire to Mr. Trudeau's pledge, "The Just Society," but that can only be realized when Jesus Christ comes again to set up His kingdom of peace and plenty on planet earth. Then, and then only, will His model prayer be answered: "Thy kingdom come. Thy will be done in earth, as it is in heaven" (Matt. 6:10).

Meanwhile, only Christ can transform the individual. Freddie Prinz's mother is currently instituting a five million dollar lawsuit against Freddie's psychiatrist for not saving Freddie's life. We just can't seem to realize that only Jesus Christ can give life; and only He can save people from death. Ohio psychiatrist, Dr. William H. Holloway, president of the International Transactional Analysis Association, stunned many recently when he admitted candidly: "We don't really know if anything in psychiatry works." Small wonder, then, that Dr. E. Fuller Torrey has written a book on *The Death of Psychiatry*.

Meanwhile, we do *know* that Jesus saves.

Sam Hamilton is a big, handsome man from Toronto. He and his wife were moderately successful. But, like millions of other moderns, they were secular pagans deep into the rat-race for happiness. One Sunday afternoon last year he was in a bar. The subject of religion came up. After a loud conversation, he went home. Dropping into a chair, he saw TV Guide open to the page advertising "Agape." He turned it on and saw Bev Shea singing: "Sweet Hour of Prayer" and heard the message preached. He felt a strong urge to give his life to Jesus. So he did. His wife was also born again. Now both are living dynamic lives for Christ, already having led many other people directly and indirectly into experiences of spiritual new birth.

This leads me to state that being born again inevitably leads to spiritual reproduction. When the maniac of Gadara was met by Christ and was transformed, he implored "him [Jesus] that he might be with him. Howbeit Jesus suffered him not, but saith unto him, Go home to thy friends, and tell them how great things the Lord hath done for thee" (Mark 5:18, 19).

John Nabor, winner of four gold medals at the Montreal Olympics, gave a testimony in one of our crusades a few weeks later. He told how Ric Careno had come to his high school in Woodbridge, California, on October 2, 1972, and led him to Christ. "There," said Nabor, "was where I was born again." I was present the night in 1969 when Ric Careno, Hell's Angel and heroin addict, came from a four-day high in a garbage container, to be converted in a Graham Crusade at Anaheim. And Ric led John Nabor to Christ. Later, from the Olympic platform, John Nabor told a billion viewers on television that he was Christ's. I suspect no one in history has ever spoken for Christ to so many at once.

When one becomes a born-again believer and is obedient to Christ to lead others to Him, ideally he becomes, not just an adder, but a multiplier. In the New Testament the proclaimers of Christ began with one—John the Baptist. Then there were 2, then 10, then 12, then 70, then 120, then 3,000, then 5,000, then 10,000 times 10,000. Leighton Ford was addressing the Evangelical Fellowship of Canada in May, 1977, and reasoned that if Billy Graham were to keep preaching Christ until he was 91, with the same results he is currently seeing, one million, six hundred thousand would be added to Christ's Church. On the other hand, if his brother Melvin, a farmer, led one person to Christ in one year, and that person in turn led one person to Christ the following year, and each lived for 33 years, each new convert annually leading someone else to Christ, within a generation the current population of the earth (4 billion) could be born again. If the population of the earth had by then doubled, it would take only one additional year for the 8 billion to be Christians.

Of course this is hypothetical. But it demonstrates the possibilities of spiritual reproduction through multiplication. St. Paul thought a lot about this principle late in his ministry. He wrote to Timothy, in the last epistle which we have of his in the New Testament: "Thou therefore, my son, be strong in the grace that is in Christ Jesus. And the things that thou hast heard of me among many witnesses, the same commit thou to faithful men, who shall be able to teach others also" (2 Tim. 2:1, 2).

When we were in the Philippines recently, it was my privilege to preach nightly for ten days in a stadium in the capital city. Coming forward to give his life to Jesus Christ one night was a great, sturdy man with a smiling face. He had been born in Mainland China and was a chemist by profession. Before escaping through Hong Kong, he looked for a Messiah. He tried Confucius, Buddha and Mao Tse Tung. Now in the crusade, he came forward to begin with Christ. And as Jesus arose on the horizon of his life, William Kho's face looked like sunrise at the equator. The next night he was back with his son, a lawyer, who came forward to give his life to Christ. The following evening they had eight other lawyers with them, all of whom came to acclaim Jesus Christ as their Messiah. I heard later that they were studying the Bible and getting the message of Christ out to others. They were part of Christ's multiplication table.

Does individual rebirth actually transform world society? No. Only when Christ comes again will this happen! Like many theologians, sociologists, politicians and philosophers, I have spent much time pondering how we could improve our world, only to see overall, social conditions deteriorating.

But having said this, I would like to stress that every born-again Christian is to give everything he has, evangelistically and socially, to contribute to the elevation and enrichment of society.

Look back into Church history. Many centuries ago Saint Basil exhorted believers: "The bread in your box belongs to the hungry; the cloak in your closet belongs to the naked; the shoes you do not wear belong to the barefoot; the money in your vault belongs to the destitute." William Penn, the father of Pennsylvania, one day stated his life philosophy: "I expect to pass through life but once. If therefore there be any kindness I can show, or any good thing I can do to any fellow being, let me do it now, and not defer or neglect, as I shall not pass this way again."

Dr. John Vanier is the son of our late Governor General of Canada. He has served our country as a physician, a psychiatrist, a professor, and now, since his remarkable surrender to Christ, as a great preacher of Jesus. He sometimes speaks in huge meetings. But it is the one-to-one testimonies he tells about which are the most moving. Frequently, he simply puts his hand on a Christless person's shoulder, looks into his eyes and says, "Jesus." And into the empty void of their lives comes Jesus to occupy them with all His fullness and joy.

Dr. Vanier's social contribution is his compassion and care for the mentally retarded, a section of the community which he realized was nearly totally bypassed by the Church. So, throughout the free world he has established hundreds of villages in which they are given total social and spiritual attention and care.

To me, having devoted a sizable percentage of my doctoral dissertation at Oxford to this theme, there is no doubt that for two centuries born-again believers have been in the forefront of social concern. Stephan Grellet and Elizabeth Fry worked in prison reform. John Howard and William Wilberforce brought the abolition of slavery. Lord Shaftesbury and Keir Hardie struggled for labor reform. Dr. Barnardo and William Booth went to the orphans, the social rejects, the refugees and the sub-tenth of the great industrial cities. Henry Dunant started his Red Cross. And World Vision is taking food, clothing and medicine into the war-torn and starving areas of a heartbreaking world.

The London Free Press recently stated that "one Canadian or American child uses enough food and natural resources to support 100 children in Bangladesh." That is nearly unbelievable. But it is indicative of the apparent inequities of our world. According to a United Nations Commission, 780 million children throughout the world have fatally deficient food supplies. Recently, Professor Neal Stoskopf of Guelph University stunned a conference with the announcement that, as a crop scientist, he was convinced that a billion people within a year "could die of starvation ... if favorable weather (worldwide) does not return to promote food production." So the situation is grave and very depressing. Jesus was so concerned about hunger that He turned two fish and five loaves into a miracle meal for a multitude of 5,000. Every Christian should be concerned about the hunger, the violence and the social perils in our world.

Ottawa native, the Rev. Morgan Thompson, wrote to me about Jimmy Watkins, who had given his life to Christ in a crusade. "Having made enough money in insurance to live on, within a couple of weeks after the crusade he had rented an old building downtown at his own expense and had begun a Rescue Mission. He now serves 1,000 meals every month to destitute people who need spiritual truth even more than physical substances. People continue to find the Lord as Saviour in that run-down old building because God stirred the heart of one man."

Recently my friend, Rev. Harold Salem, reminded me of a crusade I conducted in Aberdeen in a football stadium. Among the hundreds who were born again was a beautiful little girl named Jean Feiock. She was then 9 or 10 years old. She has since earned her M.A. in speech therapy. She has a brilliant mind, which she has put to work teaching those with speech impediments how to speak, working out new techniques in this needy field. Her intellectual, as well as her spiritual, dedication springs from that experience with Christ which she had back in the sixties when she was reborn.

In 1975, I received a phone call from Mark Johnson, director of a delinquent boys' home in Guelph, Ontario. Mark told me it all began in Britain on December 22, 1958, when he and his wife gave their lives to Christ. He recalled that I had said to him that night at the point of his surrender to Jesus: "Mark, if you'd give your heart to the Lord, what a mark you'd make on this world for Christ." He did and now he's doing his bit to be a lifter in a sinking world.

It was a century ago that David Thoreau wrote: "There are a thousand hacking at the branches of evil, to one who is striking at the roots." The only One capable of coping with the roots of society is Jesus Christ. Only He can tear up the wheat and the tares and sort out society in a new earth.

Chapter 11

Where Does Being Born Again Lead?

Millions of people hesitate on the brink of being born again because of their fear of where it will lead them. Implicit to Saul of Tarsus being born again as Paul the Apostle was his surrender to the will of God. This is an inescapable sequel to everyone who comes to Christ for salvation. Paul defined the doings of a born-again believer as a life of "understanding what the will of the Lord is" (Eph. 5:17) and then doing it.

The will of God is the believer's total concern.

What is the surest way to know the will of God? The willingness and resolution to do it. Said Jesus: "If any man will do his will, he shall know" (John 7:17). As a Christian you can be absolutely sure of one thing: Christ has a work for you to do which no one else can do as He wants you to do it. Reverend and Mrs. Victor McMannus told me recently of their former maid, Angela Watson. My wife and I were staying with them the first winter we were married. I had apparently said to Angela: "Do you know Jesus Christ as your Saviour and Lord?" Replying that she didn't, but would like to, she knelt down then and there and gave her life to Christ. Shortly after, she went to the Faith Mission Bible Training Institute in Edinburgh, through nurses training, and then to Nigeria. There she has been leading people to Christ and helping in the healing of bodies for eighteen years.

It seems to me from the Scriptures that one of the surest evidences that someone has been born again is that he immediately feels it is God's will to reach someone else for Christ.

Olga Brady's father had been a German gold miner and her mother was a Filipino beauty queen. She had married an American lawyer, and the couple lived in one of the most palatial mansions in Upper Luzon. But suddenly, Brady died and Olga grew bitter and morose. They had had no children because they wanted to be swingers in the social circuit. So Olga was overtaken by a sense of complete alienation and despair. She felt that the Filippinos treated her as a European, and the Europeans treated her as if she were Filippino. She locked herself into her house alone and vegetated. She often thought of suicide. Like Frank Sinatra's song, she just wanted to curl up and die. Then one day, a knock came on her door. It was a kindly person inviting her to a gospel meeting in the University of Baguio gymnasium. She came only to escape her melancholy. Sitting up in the balcony, she heard a knock at her heart's door. It was Jesus. Would she open her life to Him? She decided she would. And she did. And the very next night she brought her doctor to the service. He, too, was born again. And when we left Mile High Baguio in the Northern Philippines, it seemed that Olga Brady was lighting up the whole spiritual sky with her glowing testimony to the power of the Risen Christ.

But, in case someone should get the impression that being born again is all fun and games, let me hasten to stress that it is also a spiritual battle.

The Christian will never be happy or content in a state of spiritual defeat. He will strive for the mastery. He will fight the good fight of faith.

I serve as Chancellor of Richmond College, and our Biology professor is Dr. Norman Martyn. He is also an Anglican rector of a parish near Peterborough where Joe Scriven, over a century ago, wrote the most familiar words ever written in Canada. Joe was a missionary from Ireland, working among our Iroquois Indians when he was joined by his Irish fiance. Just before the wedding, she was killed in an ice accident. Joe buried her with his own hands and a broken heart. A year later, in a letter to his mother, he reflected:

> What a friend we have in Jesus,
> All our sins and griefs to bear!
> What a privilege to carry
> Everything to God in prayer!
> Have we trials and temptations?
> Is there trouble anywhere?
> We should never be discouraged,
> Take it to the Lord in prayer.

Joe Scriven was on the road to triumph, even though for him, as for all, there were times when the road was rough.

Where else does the born-again experience lead? Into the strengthening of Christian marriages and Christ-centered homes. In Ephesians 5, St. Paul taught that in being "followers of God, as dear children ... as the church is subject unto Christ, so let the wives be to their own husbands in every thing. Husbands, love your wives, even as Christ loved the church, and gave himself for it" (vv. 1, 24, 25), and "Children obey your parents in the Lord ... and, ye fathers, provoke not your children to wrath: but bring them up in the nurture and admonition of the Lord" (6:1, 4).

Here in Canada one in four marriages ends in divorce. Only one in twelve marriages ended in divorce when we entered our second century as a nation in 1967. In the United States, the divorce rate has gone up as much in the last four years as in the previous ten. And ten times as many couples register that they are living common-law now, as a decade ago. This effects nearly everyone sooner or later, because everyone is born into a family, and sooner or later 97 percent of men and 96 percent of women marry. Nine out of ten of both sexes attach maximum priority in life to a happy marriage. Many take marriage all too lightly: a television program is frivolously entitled: "How to Survive a Marriage!" A magazine cover story is entitled: "Hooked on a Married Man!", while a columnist cracks: "The trouble with marriage is that the whole thing has given divorce a bad name." In the name of women being liberated, judges are now beginning to grant the custody of children to adulterous wives, while 20 percent of single-parent families in North America are now headed up by the father—up 300 percent.

Is divorce really as frivolous or glamorous as many in the media make out? Canadian TV star Michele Finney lamented recently over her "lousy marriage and the rotten divorce," which lead to so many "frustrations" and "bitterness." Joane Carson goes public in relating how divorce from Johnny felt: "You both lose... that's the strongest thing that comes through, the fact that you've both lost. There is the agony of picking up the pieces... there is no way to go through divorce easily. I don't care who wants out, both people go through their own private hells. It touches every single part of your life from skin to gut level."

And divorce costs all of us money—in tax dollars. In Ontario, we pay for 40% of the divorces trans-acted in this province, not to mention the millions it costs to support the abandoned children who are casualties of these divorces. Jesus Christ, when He was here on earth, was very concerned about the home. He was born into a home. His first miracle was at a marriage ceremony. He often healed broken hearts by raising a dead son to his mother, or a dead daughter to her father. And when He was on the cross, He cared for His mother, Mary, by committing her to the custody of John the Apostle.

Is your marriage on the Rock, or on the rocks? Doctor George Crane, M.D., Ph.D., the clinical col-umnist in newspapers throughout North America, has calculated that when a married couple are active together in the same church they have about a 50 times greater chance of avoiding divorce; and that only one in 500 marriages breaks up where there is a family altar. It is a truism in this final quarter of the 20th century that the family that prays together stays together.

I received a letter the other day from a man in Idaho. He told me, "Because of my neglect of my spiritual life, I now find myself separated from my wife. I put myself first and finished last. My wife put God first and finished first. I had just put the two lit-tle girls down for a nap and switched channels on the TV and I knew if I watched, there would be a mes-sage for me." There was, and he says: "I prayed the sinner's prayer."

On a Friday night, during a recent meeting in Cal-ifornia among those who came forward to be born again in Christ was a handsome 18-year-old, Tom Har-ris. He attended nightly thereafter until Tuesday.

After the service he came up and told me he was flying back home to the Midwest in a few hours. Tom had left home at 16. Not once had he contacted his parents. Instead, he got into a ripoff swindle, peddaling fake magazine subscriptions and spending the money on a life that included shooting heroin between his toes. Now, with Christ, he had phoned his family. His folks were so glad to hear from him that they wired him a ticket to come home and he had come to tell me that he was on his way.

John and Julia Mays had given up on their marriage and separated. One night at a gospel meeting, without either knowing of the other's presence, they both came forward and were born again. Then they saw each other. And they went home to live together, to love each other and to serve Christ. That was ten years ago, and they're still with Christ.

Being born again gives us a new love for our families.

Finally, being born again leads us into a triumphant homegoing to be with Christ. I saw a note in *The Toronto Globe and Mail* which read: "Work for the Lord. The pay is not much, but the retirement plan is out of this world!" St. John wrote of those of us who have been born again: "Beloved, now are we the sons of God, and it doth not yet appear what we shall be: but we know that, when he shall appear, we shall be like him, for we shall see him as he is" (1 John 3:2).

When I lived in Oxford, England, I drove down to what might have been the poorest and most squalid coal mining village in Wales to preach each night for a week in a tiny chapel. Each day I'd go house to house and ask the dwellers, "Does Jesus live here?" If he didn't, I'd try to explain how He'd like to move in and transform their lives.

One afternoon I was knocking on doors and came

to one which was ajar. When I knocked, it swung open. There in the shadows was a worn-out old man of 80 years with partially patched coal-dust saturated overalls. His off-white whiskers matched his mane of grizzley, grey hair which hung over his tired eyes blinking above a toothless smile. He knew me. He had hobbled around to the little chapel the night before. With lungs eaten out by a lifetime of inhaling coal dust, he squeaked, "Come in." With a big, rough, shaky hand he shook mine and led me over to a creaky table, sitting me down on a wobbly bench beside it. Off to his right was a coal fire and hanging over it a black-coated chain suspending a soot-covered kettle. Removing it, he poured its contents into two rusty tin cups of tea leaves. A shake of sugar and a splash of milk later, tea was served. With a dull knife, worn nearly in half, he hacked off a couple of pieces of bread from a nearly spent loaf, and squeezed chunks of cheese into them. It was the miners' staff of life. He wanted me to eat and drink with him, and I did. But when I asked him if Jesus lived here, he replied that He didn't. However, since the meeting the night before, he'd thought of nothing else. His wife was dead and his children were long gone and hardly ever came to see him. How could he invite Jesus into his life and know that he was His? I said, "Friend, just as when I knocked on your door, you asked me to come in and sit down and eat with you, so Jesus knocks on your heart's door, and when you invite Him to do so, He comes into your life and sups with you and shares life eternal with you." There and then he asked Jesus to come into his heart. When I left, there was the freshness of new spiritual life on his face. He had been well and truly born again.

Early the next morning, I felt the urge to go around and see my old friend again, and when I turned into his street, there was a slow, soupy rain falling. When I reached his grubby door, it was tightly shut. After knocking and hearing no movement, I looked through the window. The drape was drawn, but not quite all the way. Through the opening, I saw a plain pine coffin, the kind the British Government provides for those who can't buy their own. The lid was up and there was my friend, and on his face I thought I saw an expression of peace which read, "To live is Christ, and to die is gain."

Chapter 12

How Can You Be Born Again Now?

If you feel the Holy Spirit speaking in your heart and saying that this is your day of decision, you have an immediate appointment with God. When Jesus passed through Jericho for the last time, en route to Jerusalem and Calvary, He looked up into a sycamore tree, and there crouched a little man. Jesus did not wave to him, wink at him and suggest: "Hey there, how about being a follower of mine— sometime? Don't rush. Think it over. See how it sits with your family or whether it squares with your friends. Get your lawyer's advice. Check it out with your doctor and perhaps your psychiatrist. See what your wife thinks!" That is not what Jesus said. Instead, He commanded, "Zaccheus, make haste, and come down, for today I must abide at thy house." It's now or never. It's salvation or spiritual suicide. It's come to heaven, or go to hell.

In Hebrews 11:25-26, we read of how Moses' "choosing" of Christ took place. It was when he heard God's voice and saw His flaming light that he opted for "the reproach of Christ." Where did it happen? I believe that, for Moses, it was by that burning bush; for Gideon, it was under that oak tree; for James and John, it was down by that sea; for the Samaritan harlot from Scarlet Street, it was out by that well; for Zaccheus, it was halfway between that limb on that sycamore tree and the ground; for the thief, it was on that cross next to Jesus; for the Ethiopian nobleman, it was right in that chariot; for Paul the apostle, it was on that Damascus Road; for the Philippian jailer, it was right in that prison.

Time magazine recorded recently of how Jimmy Snow, son of Halifax's beloved Hank Snow, the world-famous country music star, gave his life to Christ and became a nationally known preacher. Eighteen years ago Jimmy was pulling down big money, but as he says, "I drank it all up. . . . I decided I'd had enough . . . women, liquor and pills were destroying me. I went to the front yard in the middle of the night and asked God to take me. I knew right away." Jimmy Snow keeps on his desk a picture of that spot in the front yard where he was born again.

Today, *where* you are and just *as* you are *is God's time, place* and *state* for you to be born again.

To be born again you start by acknowledging to Christ that you are a sinner. Jesus told us that He had "not come to call the righteous, but sinners, to repentance" (Matt. 9:12-13). So you must begin, just as a doctor diagnoses his patient, by acknowledging that you have violated God's laws and have separated yourself from God by doing so.

The next thing you must do is to repent of all your sins. This means that you must determine to have a wholehearted change of attitude about sin. It means turning from your sins.

Having repented, you are now ready to receive Christ as Savior.

You may recall that President Gerald Ford was having a press conference in the East Room of the

White House just before the 1976 election. The announcer's voice boomed out to the gathered press, "The President of the United States!" They heard a knock at the door. But the president, the most powerful man on earth, was not entering. The knob had fallen off the outside of the door. Spiritually, Jesus, the most powerful person in the universe, wants to enter your life. But, He has left the knob on the inside of your heart's door. Only you can ask Him to come in.

Next, you place your whole trust in Christ as your only Saviour. You allow Him to become Lord, King— everything.

When you have repented and received Christ, you must declare what you have done. This declaration is an integral part of a spiritual transaction with Christ. Jesus told us, "Whosoever therefore shall confess me before men, him will I confess also before my Father which is in heaven" (Matt. 10:32).

Whether you are on a plane, or bus, or reading this in your home, a hospital, or a jail cell does not really matter. What does matter is that you make certain you are born again. If there is any doubt in your mind, may I suggest you go to prayer immediately, and pray something like this:

"God be merciful to me a sinner. And save me now for Christ's sake. I now repent of all my sin. I gratefully acknowledge that Jesus died in my place so that I may have the privilege of receiving Him as my Lord and Savior. I receive Him into my heart and life, and put my entire trust in Him to forgive my sins and give me the gift of eternal life. Amen."

If your repentance is genuine, and your trust in Christ is sincere, be assured that God will keep His promises by accepting you as one of His spiritual children. He will give you inner assurance that you have been born again.

I invite you to write me a letter. I will send you a reply and some counseling materials which will help you in your spiritual life.

Just write to me:

Dr. John Wesley White
Winnipeg, Canada

or

John Wesley White
c/o Billy Graham Association
Minneapolis, Minnesota
55403